Cambridge Elements ≡

Elements in Current Archaeological Tools and Techniques
edited by
Hans Barnard
Cotsen Institute of Archaeology
Willeke Wendrich
Polytechnic University of Turin

BIOARCHAEOLOGY OF INFANTS AND CHILDREN

L. Creighton Avery
University of Toronto

Shaftesbury Road, Cambridge CB2 8EA, United Kingdom

One Liberty Plaza, 20th Floor, New York, NY 10006, USA

477 Williamstown Road, Port Melbourne, VIC 3207, Australia

314–321, 3rd Floor, Plot 3, Splendor Forum, Jasola District Centre, New Delhi – 110025, India

103 Penang Road, #05–06/07, Visioncrest Commercial, Singapore 238467

Cambridge University Press is part of Cambridge University Press & Assessment, a department of the University of Cambridge.

We share the University's mission to contribute to society through the pursuit of education, learning and research at the highest international levels of excellence.

www.cambridge.org
Information on this title: www.cambridge.org/9781009543668

DOI: 10.1017/9781009543675

© L. Creighton Avery 2025

This publication is in copyright. Subject to statutory exception and to the provisions of relevant collective licensing agreements, no reproduction of any part may take place without the written permission of Cambridge University Press & Assessment.

When citing this work, please include a reference to the DOI 10.1017/9781009543675

First published 2025

A catalogue record for this publication is available from the British Library.

ISBN 978-1-009-54366-8 Hardback
ISBN 978-1-009-54364-4 Paperback
ISSN 2632-7031 (online)
ISSN 2632-7023 (print)

Additional resources for this publication at www.cambridge.com/avery

Cambridge University Press & Assessment has no responsibility for the persistence or accuracy of URLs for external or third-party internet websites referred to in this publication and does not guarantee that any content on such websites is, or will remain, accurate or appropriate.

For EU product safety concerns, contact us at Calle de José Abascal, 56, 1°, 28003 Madrid, Spain, or email eugpsr@cambridge.org

Bioarchaeology of Infants and Children

Elements in Current Archaeological Tools and Techniques

DOI: 10.1017/9781009543675
First published online: June 2025

L. Creighton Avery
University of Toronto

Author for correspondence: L. Creighton Avery, creighton.avery@utoronto.ca

Abstract: The study of infant, child, and adolescent remains (non-adult remains) is a topic of growing interest within the fields of archaeology and bioarchaeology. Many published volumes and articles delve into the experiences of childhood and what these small remains may tell us about life, more broadly, in the past. For those interested in exploring infant and child remains, it is an exciting period as more methods and approaches are constantly being incorporated into the archaeological toolkit. This Element introduces the reader to the topic and to common methodological approaches used to consider non-adult remains from archaeological contexts. With this toolkit in hand, readers will be able to begin their own explorations and analyses of non-adult human remains within archaeological contexts.

Keywords: bioarchaeology, childhood, growth, diet, trauma

© L. Creighton Avery 2025

ISBNs: 9781009543668 (HB), 9781009543644 (PB), 9781009543675 (OC)
ISSNs: 2632-7031 (online), 2632-7023 (print)

Contents

1 Origins of the Study of Childhood   1

2 Entering the Archaeological Record   7

3 Skeletal Age and Social Age   12

4 Sex and Gender   20

5 Growth Disruptions   27

6 Diet and Feeding   35

7 Trauma and Child Abuse   39

8 Adolescence   43

9 Future Directions   50

10 Recording Forms   53

    Bibliography   63

1 Origins of the Study of Childhood

The "birth" of the study of childhood in the past is a story told in many other places (e.g., Halcrow and Tayles 2008, 2011, Kamp 2001, Lewis 2007, Mays et al. 2017), but is worth telling again for those new to the subdiscipline. The origin of the study of childhood is often attributed to the 1960s publication by Phillip Ariès (1962) entitled *Centuries of Childhood: A Social History of Family Life*. In this text, Ariès defined childhood as a modern invention and a period of overindulged dependency that, prior to the modern period, did not exist as a stage in the human life course. Instead, he claimed that parents in the past were unsympathetic and detached from their children, essentially treating them as miniature adults (Ariès 1962) (Figure 1).

The publication by Ariès (1962) drew staunch criticisms (e.g., see Wilson 1980 for discussion), as individuals claimed that this was a gross oversimplification of experiences in the past. To investigate, or perhaps with the intention to disprove these claims, researchers began investigating how children were perceived in past societies (e.g., Hammond and Hammond 1981). However, these early studies were not necessarily focused on understanding the lives of children directly, but rather explored adult perceptions of childhood.

In the 1970s, feminist-inspired approaches to anthropology called for the more purposeful and intentional inclusion of women in archaeological studies (e.g., Claassen 1992; Gero & Conkey 1991). In addition to "finding women," feminist anthropologists also called attention to other underrepresented groups, like children, and began to investigate these groups in relation to the dominant adult male perspective (Baxter 2008, 2019; Lewis 2007). In this vein, Grete Lillehammer's 1989 paper, "A Child Is Born," suggested – perhaps, for the first time – that we could use burials, artifacts, ethnographies, and osteology to gain insight into the relationship the child had with its physical environment and adult world. In this paper, Lillehammer (1989) provided a call to action for other archaeologists and anthropologists to consider not only the conditions of childhood, but the lived experiences of children and infants, contextualizing data to provide insights into life in the past.

Following these seminal works, the anthropological study of childhood in the past has flourished, as more researchers engage with this topic of research. No single book could capture the diversity of approaches, both methodological and theoretical, nor the questions and hypotheses that drive bioarchaeological research into infants and children. What can be said is that anthropologists now recognize that childhood as much more than a biological age of overindulged dependency, and characterize it as a series of social and cultural events and experiences that make up a child's life. As this period of life is defined by these social and cultural

Figure 1 Child's sarcophagus with a procession of Dionysian cupids by a Greek workshop from the Isola Sacra, Via Severiana (2nd century CE). Photo by the author; original sarcophagus at Ostia Antica, Italy.

events, however, we cannot simply transpose our own views of childhood directly onto the past but need to investigate them within each cultural and temporal context.

The Bioarchaeology of Childhood

In biological anthropology, non-adult remains (i.e., developmentally immature skeletal remains)[1] were described as having "little anthropological value" by Earnest Hooton in 1930 (Hooton 1930, 15). This sentiment was not unique at the time but reflected the state of biological anthropology in the early 20th century. At this point, research methods focused on metrics or measurements of the body to try to find differences between populations. Meanwhile, publications utilized descriptive writing, describing the disease or condition visible, rather than trying to understand where it came from or why some people were more affected than others, or what the presence of this disease in the past might mean about life in the past, more broadly. Hooton (1930) continued that, in this world of metrics and descriptive writing, the physical remains of non-adults were fragile and often poorly preserved, so they did not offer the same academic value or meaning that a fully articulated and mature skeleton could.

When biological anthropologists did consider non-adult remains, it was often with the intent of establishing methods to estimate age and sex, rather than asking questions about childhood health or agency (Lewis 2007, 10). While these studies (e.g., Schour and Massler 1941; Olivier and Pineau 1960) now

---

[1] Within this Element the terms "infant" and "child" refer to socially constructed views incorporating biological age, physical capabilities, and social positions. Meanwhile, the term "non-adult" will refer to developmentally immature skeletal remains, isolated from their social and cultural context (similar texts often use the terminology "sub-adult" or "juvenile remains").

form foundational pieces for the study of childhood, they were ultimately limited in scope, listing and describing conditions rather than implementing theoretical frameworks to better gain a more nuanced view of life in the past.

The pattern of metrics and descriptive writing started to change some thirty years later, when researchers began to link non-adult growth patterns with poor health during life (e.g., Johnston 1962). Shortly afterwards, biological anthropologists began to examine measurements of long bones to understand growth and stunting in past populations. Once again, these studies were not particularly focused on learning more about childhood experiences, but rather used conditions of childhood as a proxy for the overall health of past populations (Lewis 2007; Saunders 2008). It is important to note, that many of these studies were conducted on Indigenous remains, often without the informed consent of descent groups; this is an approach that should not be replicated today.

Progress in the study of childhood, however, or at least the study of non-adult skeletal remains, came to a pause in the 1980s when Buikstra and Cook (1980) stated that studies of children were hindered by poor preservation, lack of recovery, and small sample sizes. Subsequent papers focused on this lack of preservation of non-adults, in some ways, as an explanatory factor as to why they were not investigating non-adults more closely (e.g., Von Endt and Ortner 1984). Lewis (2007, 12) states that this assumption continues today, limiting further investigations.

Then, in the same year that Grete Lillehammer wrote "A Child Is Born," Goodman and Armelagos (1989) suggested that children under the age of five are particularly sensitive to environmental and cultural insults. So, once again, researchers started looking at non-adult remains to learn about their growth and health, in order to learn more about the communities in which they lived. However, more than just using biological data from non-adult remains as a proxy for adult health and well-being, Goodman and Armelagos (1989) established the biocultural approach (discussed later in the Element) and incorporated this theoretical framework into their studies, pushing beyond descriptive research into learning more about life in the past.

A rise in research incorporating non-adult skeletal remains prompted the publication of several foundational pieces of work, including Scheuer and Black's (2000) *Developmental Juvenile Osteology* and Lewis' (2007) *The Bioarchaeology of Children*. There are also specific associations (e.g., the Society for the Study of Childhood in the Past [SSCIP]) and academic journals (e.g., *Childhood in the Past*) that promote and publish newly developing research on the topic of infants and children in the past. Today, studies incorporating non-adult remains employ questions that are more socially driven, attempting to understand how children were viewed and socially treated in the past, how they interacted with (and related to) their own world, and how they contributed to the communities around them (Halcrow and Tayles 2008; Baker 2018 in Beauchesne and Agarwal 2018; Thompson *et al.* 2014). As a result, children are being included in a wider range of studies than ever before.

This Element incorporates some of the foundational methods and approaches used in the bioarchaeological study of infants and children, with associated recording sheets available at the end of the Element (fillable forms also are available for download online).[2]

Theory in Childhood Bioarchaeology

Theory is an analytical tool used to help explain certain phenomena or processes. Within biological anthropology, the intentional use of theoretical frameworks can allow a researcher to move beyond descriptive reports to contextualized and informed conclusions. In many ways, theory is the lens through which you can view your data. Hypothetically, this means you can use the same dataset with different theoretical frameworks and, ultimately, get different perspectives or insights from the data.

Bioarchaeological research today relies on the incorporation of theoretical frameworks, like the biocultural approach. Although the application of theory is not always explicit in research, it is often present. However, I would argue that being explicit with which theoretical framework you are using enables others to understand where you are coming from, and where you are going with your research question and analysis of data. Identifying and describing which theoretical framework underpins your analyses can also help reveal potential biases in your research, which enables the reader to understand your perspective and why you interpreted or considered some items in particular ways. With this point in mind, key theoretical frameworks are summarized in what follows; but texts also are available that delve deeply into this topic. For further discussions regarding use of theory in bioarchaeology, see Cheverko and colleagues' (2021) *Theoretical Approaches in Bioarchaeology* or Geller's (2021) *Theorizing Bioarchaeology*.

Biocultural Approach

In biological anthropology, the most often employed theoretical framework is the biocultural approach. First articulated in the medical anthropology literature, biological anthropological interpretations of data were found by Goodman and Leatherman (1998) too often to be empty of social content, and as a result,

---

[2] www.cambridge.com/avery

interpretations were reductionistic, irrelevant, or simply wrong, especially when considered by other disciplines in anthropology. Meanwhile, at the time, biological anthropologists often found that the theories used by cultural anthropologists were "excessively relativistic navel gazing, unimportant, and antiscientific" (Goodman and Leatherman 1998, p. 7). Within this growing divide, biological anthropology was moving further and further away from theory. As a result, biological anthropologists were seemingly stuck, and could only offer descriptions of past skeletons instead of talking about health or lived experiences.

The biocultural approach seeks to break the dichotomy between biology and culture and places the emphasis on how sociocultural and political-economic processes affect and influence the biology of people (Goodman and Leatherman 1998). The biocultural approach is unique, as it crosses sub-disciplines to discern experiences that affect the human body but can otherwise remain archaeologically or historically invisible (Zuckerman and Armelagos 2011). For example, while paleobotany may be able to distinguish the types of food available at a site, by studying the human remains researchers can explore rates of dental disease. Subsequently, through the lens of the biocultural approach, researchers can better understand the various social, political, and economic variables that influenced access to material resources (e.g., Avery *et al.* 2019).

Biological anthropologists now incorporate a wide range of theoretical frameworks, although many may fall under the umbrella of the biocultural approach. Three such approaches are included here; however, researchers are encouraged to consider a range of theoretical approaches to identify which approach suits their own context, conditions, and questions. This may include feminist or queer theories, life history theories, evolutionary theories, and more.

Embodiment

In biological anthropology, the skeleton is often viewed as two separate entities: (1) the physical remains that are analyzed and quantified, and (2) the representation of cultural ideas (Joyce, 2005). The theoretical framework of embodiment emphasizes that these two bodies are not distinct, but rather, that cultural ideas are expressed within the physical remains (Jimenez et al. 2009). In other words, habitual and severe actions can leave marks on our skeleton. Biological anthropologists then identify and investigate those skeletal marks, and through the theory of embodiment, work to understand what lived experiences contributed to those marks. The most obvious of these *embodied* marks are body modifications, such as cranial modification, which represent the direct incorporation of cultural ideas into physical remains. These are often used to express cultural identity, kinship groups, or status (Tiesler 2014). However, less obvious markers of a person's lived experiences may also become embodied into their physical remains.

For example, Maass (2023) uses a biocultural approach to consider the experiences of children recovered from a colonial plantation, and how the status of enslaved children shaped their embodied experiences within colonial society. Also, Nikitovic (2017) considers how social identity becomes embedded in the physical bodies of children among ancestral and historic Puebloans of the American Southwest.

A few caveats are worth mentioning, however. The first is that not all cultural ideas or markers of human life will become imprinted on bones. These include soft tissue changes or modifications, short-term changes that may be no less meaningful to the individual, low-impact changes, or emotional and mental changes. Additionally, individuals may assume multiple identities throughout their lifetime, and as their identities change, so too might their cultural and social experiences. Thus, it is important to consider the cross-cutting variables of identity, as well as identities that change and shift across the human life course.

Developmental Origins of Health and Disease

The developmental origins of health and disease (DOHaD) approach demonstrates that environmental exposures early in life (particularly during the *in utero* period) not only have immediate consequences for growth and development, but can also permanently influence health and vulnerability to disease later in life (Baker *et al.* 1989; Gowland 2015; Gamble and Bentley 2022; Gowland and Caldwell 2022). Traditionally, DOHaD has been applied in medical research and nutritional studies of living people but has more recently been applied to bioarchaeological studies.

For example, Garland (2020) assessed the frequency and timing of early life stressors and mortality risk for Indigenous Guale in Spanish Florida (17th century). Assessing enamel micro-growth disruptions, Gowland (2020) found that individuals with early forming *and* frequent enamel disruptions had an increased risk of an early death. Meanwhile, Samantha Holder and colleagues (2021) examined linear enamel hypoplastic defects and adult stature in the remains of Napoleonic soldiers (see Section 5 for more details regarding growth disruptions). They hypothesized that stress in early life growth and development would have a negative impact on growth outcomes in adulthood. However, Holder and colleagues (2021) found that the results were actually much more nuanced, speaking to confounding effects of catch-up growth, resilience, and plasticity in human growth.

Mother–Infant Nexus

While DOHaD speaks to the long-term consequences of poor early childhood growth and development, the mother–infant nexus allows us to consider the lives of mothers as seen in the remains of infants, effectively allowing us to peer back in time. In this approach, infants are conceptualized as being contingent and relational with their mothers, rather than separate and distinct entities (Gowland and Halcrow 2020). The connection is obvious, as the *in utero* fetus and biological mother share the same body, blood, nutrition, and immune systems, and therefore when the biological mother is stressed, so too is the fetus. As a result, offspring growth and health are reflective of the varying maternal and environmental exposures encountered by the biological mother. Additionally, cultural practices or beliefs, such as dietary avoidance behaviours during pregnancy, will have biological repercussions for the developing fetus (Gowland and Halcrow 2020).

Nava (2024) uses the mother–infant nexus to consider the maternal diet, as observed in dental enamel of infants, to better understand dietary variations, mobility, health status, and growth rates of children and their mothers. Other studies have not directly stated their use of the mother–infant nexus, but evidence of the nexus can still be observed within these studies. For example, in Montreal (Canada), Gutierrez and colleagues (2021) studied patterns of weaning and stress in infants, concluding that evidence of elevated stable nitrogen values and presence of cribra orbitalia in very young infants were suggestive of maternal stress. For a more thorough look at the mother–infant nexus, see Gowland and Halcrow's (2020) edited volume *The Mother–Infant Nexus in Anthropology*.

2 Entering the Archaeological Record

In 1980, Buikstra and Cook stated that studies of non-adults are hindered by poor preservation, lack of recovery, and small sample sizes. While subsequent research has demonstrated that this is not always the case, these misconceptions have continued to haunt the bioarchaeological study of childhood (Lewis 2007).

Poor preservation is perhaps the most widely cited reason for the limited engagement with the bioarchaeological study of childhood (Lewis 2007). Researchers emphasize that, due to the porous nature of immature bones, as well as their high organic and low inorganic content, the remains of infants and children are more susceptible to decay than are adult bones (Lewis 2019). While taphonomic factors (e.g., temperature, type of soil, post-mortem disturbances) certainly have an effect on preservation, these same factors can affect preservation of adult bones (Scheuer and Black 2004; McFadden *et al.* 2022; Biehler-Gomez *et al.* 2022). Thus, one cannot simply assume that infant and child remains will be poorly preserved, as their preservation and recovery are entirely dependent on the context in which they are buried (e.g., soil, burial structure, body preparation, taphonomic processes, post-depositional perturbations).

Small sample sizes in osteological collections or archaeological sites may be attributable to other factors, including cultural practices, excavation strategies, and misidentification (described below). Gaining a thorough understanding of the representation of infant and child remains within an archaeological context can provide insights into mortality rates, fertility rates, and paleodemographic trends and patterns (McFadden *et al.* 2022; Lewis 2007). As a result, having a thorough and accurate representation of infant and child remains is an important first step to understanding a sample, population, or community.

Cultural Burial Practices

The recovery of non-adult skeletal remains may be beyond the control of archaeologists. Rather, the burial of infants and children can be influenced by social determinants and culturally relevant burial practices, as many cultures treat human infant bodies in different ways than those of other community members (Lally 2008, 29). For example, Maria Liston and Susan Rotroff (2013, 2) examined infant remains recovered from an abandoned well in the ancient Athenian Agora (2nd century BCE, Greece), suggesting that the assemblage represents a "unique window into the cultural practices associated with . . . [the] youngest, most vulnerable members [of their community]." In particular, they suggest that this burial environment was used by midwives to dispose of infants who died during childbirth, rather than being buried in a formal cemetery (Lison & Rotroff 2013). A thousand years later, Christian burial grounds often required the deceased to have been baptized prior to death in order to be buried on consecrated land. Consequently, stillborn or young infants who had not been baptized may have been buried elsewhere, or provided a clandestine burial rather than a typical or normative burial (e.g., Cootes *et al.* 2020; Gilchrist 2022). For example, *cillíní* were the designated resting places for unbaptized infants and children in Ireland (Murphy 2011). If buried elsewhere, the remains of infants and children may not be found during the excavation of the cemetery. If buried in a clandestine burial that is shallower than other graves, their burial contexts may be disturbed, limiting their archaeological presence (Lewis 2007).

In each of these contexts, cultural burial practices will limit their archaeological presence if the entire cemetery, or areas specific to infants and children, are not excavated. These alternate burial locations may not be selected for excavation, and may not be protected from future developments, meaning the skeletal remains are not recovered and can be more easily disturbed and damaged. While there may be little we can do to overcome this issue, being aware of specific cultural practices, or exploring other portions of a burial ground, may help bioarchaeologists identify and recover infant and child remains. For more examples regarding non-adult burial practices in various geographical and temporal contexts, see *Children, Death, and Burial: Archaeological Discourses*, edited by Eileen Murphy and Mélie Le Roy (2017).

Excavation Techniques

The perceived scarcity of non-adult remains in cemetery samples may also be the result of excavation practices, which have been developed for the excavation of adult remains and may be inadequate for non-adult remains (Saunders 2000; Lewis 2019). Specifically, small osteological elements may be overlooked, while unfused skeletal elements may not be identified as human remains, leading to the incomplete recovery of the individual (Baker *et al.* 2005; Scheuer and Black 2004; Saunders 2000; Sundick 1978; Lally 2008). Bioturbation of soils may also obscure smaller grave cuts, leading to the misidentification of features during archaeological excavation (McFadden *et al.* 2022).

Techniques to help ensure the recovery of infant and perinate remains include using fine mesh for screening soils. For example, Pokines and De La Paz (2016) found that using a 6.4 mm mesh resulted in 36.8 per cent recovery, while a 1.0 mm mesh resulted in the recovery of 99.8 per cent of perinate remains. Additionally, wrapping jaws prior to transportation can help retain unmineralized dentition (used for age estimates; see Section 3) (Saunders 2008). Lewis (2019) also recommends retaining the excavated soil from around a perinate burial, to be further examined in a lab setting for better controlled conditions.

Misidentification

If the graves of infants and children are located and thoroughly excavated, there are still potential issues associated with recovery, as infant and child remains due to their immature nature are frequently confused with faunal remains by non-bioarchaeologists (Buckberry 2005). For example, an amphora burial from Athens included the cremated remains (cremains) of a high-status female and additional bone that was initially identified as burned animal remains (Liston and Papadopoulos 2004). A re-examination of the material by a trained osteologist with specialization in non-adult remains, however, demonstrated that the additional bone was not faunal, but the remains of a human fetus which were likely misinterpreted due to their highly fragmentary nature, as well as the fact that the bones had been altered by the cremation process (Liston and Papadopoulos 2004, 18–19).

Reference texts dedicated to non-adult osteology help to limit these challenges and should be on hand when analyzing skeletal material. The foundational text for non-adult osteology was first published in 2000 as *Developmental Juvenile Osteology* (Scheuer and Black 2000). For the first time, this comprehensive text summarized almost 100 years of research into the non-adult skeleton, outlining what was known, and where the gaps remained. The second edition (Cunningham *et al.* 2016) includes updated and augmented illustrations and bibliography, incorporating an additional 15 years of research into non-adult remains, and to this day is the most comprehensive text on the topic of non-adult skeletal remains.

Following this text, Scheuer and Black (2004) published *The Juvenile Skeleton*, which provided a condensed version, targeting students of osteology. This publication outlines significant milestone events in the maturation of the human skeleton for a less specialized audience. Shortly afterwards, Baker *et al.* (2005) also produced a field manual and textbook for osteology courses entitled *The Osteology of Infants and Children*.

Perhaps most appropriate for in-field researchers, Schaefer and colleagues (2009) published *Juvenile Osteology: A Laboratory and Field Manual*. This brief text is designed to assist researchers by providing the methodological and mathematical tools necessary to complete their own studies rather than summarizing previous works.

While numerous sources are now available for the study of infant and child remains, the choice of text will depend on the target audience, including experience and level of detail required. If possible, the use of specialized osteoarchaeologists familiar with infant and child osteology will also be beneficial in complex cases.

Broadly speaking, human and non-human skeletal material can be differentiated based on differences in architecture and maturity. Architecturally, non-human remains may have features not present in humans, such as tails, claws, or baculum. Additionally, landmarks and articular surfaces tend to be more robust in non-human remains. Architectural differences may also be the result of different locomotion patterns or diets and are important to understand. For example, as humans are bipedal, the foramen magnum in the occipital bone is positioned inferiorly, while in quadrupeds, the foramen magnum is positioned posteriorly. Differences in the pelvis, hands, and feet may also provide indications regarding locomotion practices, and can help differentiate between human and non-human remains. With regard to teeth, human dentition, with its sharp anterior teeth and blunted posterior teeth, is suited to an omnivorous diet. Comparing these teeth with those of other animals, such as rodents or ungulates, may help differentiate between human and non-human remains.

When considering the maturity of skeletal remains, infant human remains are most likely to be misidentified as "non-human" due to their small and morphologically non-descript nature, as they are missing key features and landmarks that might help differentiate human and non-human species. The presence of growth plates and unfused epiphyses should help further identify non-adult specimens, while a completely fused/developed bone of a small size should not be mistaken for non-adult remains (Figure 2).

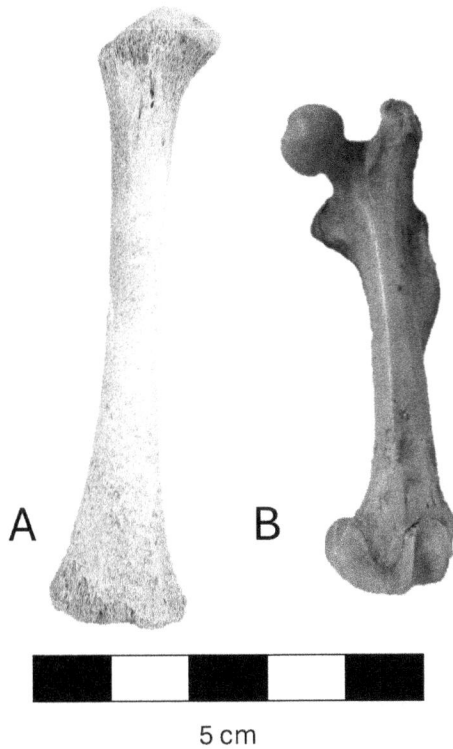

Figure 2 Photos of (A) a non-adult human femur and (B) an adult muskrat femur, illustrating differences in architecture and maturity, despite their similar size.

3 Skeletal Age and Social Age

Age is a critical axis of inquiry, forming the foundation of many bioarchaeological studies (Sofaer 2011). However, age and aging are not straightforward concepts. To fully consider age in the past, researchers may use the tripartite model of aging. In this model, age is divided into three interrelated strands (Halcrow and Tayles 2008).

1. Chronological age marks the amount of time since birth, typically measured in months or years. Within biological anthropology, this is typically accessible with the incorporation of other lines of evidence, like burial records, census records, or tombstones.
2. Biological age is associated with the development and degeneration of the human body. Within biological anthropology, biological age markers (e.g., dental development; see later discussion) have been assessed in relation to chronological age, allowing us to estimate biological age (a proxy for chronological age) through the analysis of skeletal remains. However, other biological aging events may not be as closely tied to chronological age, for example, puberty, menarche, or menopause (for further discussions of puberty, see Section 8: Adolescence).
3. Social age is related to culturally constructed age categories that encapsulate appropriate behaviours, skills, and attitudes, typically with named categories. For example, a "toddler" might have expectations of walking and talking, but not likely moving out or having a job. Meanwhile, a "teenager" might be expected to get a first job, start driving, or participate in other behaviours that are socially and culturally defined.

These three measures of age, while seemingly distinct, can often influence one another (Figure 3). The connections between chronological and biological age have already been highlighted, detailing how methods to estimate age are developed within biological anthropology. Connections between chronological age and social age can be viewed through laws passed by various countries, including the age you can vote, legal drinking age, or even the age at which you can drive a car. There is nothing particularly magical about turning 19 years old that means you can now consume alcohol (the legal age of drinking in Ontario, Canada); however, it is assumed that by this point you have reached the social maturity to make informed decisions and can be held accountable for your actions. Connections between biological and social age can be viewed through life milestones, like menarche (a female's first menstruation), which is a biological event that often serves as a marker between childhood and adulthood in the lives of young women in various cultures around the world.

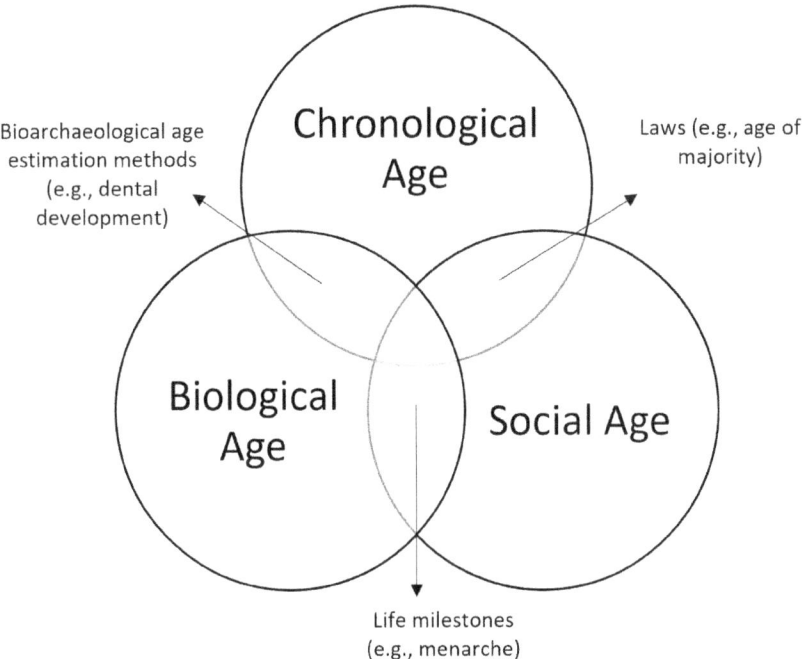

Figure 3 Tripartite model of aging including chronological, biological, and social age, along with examples where these measures of age overlap, demonstrating their intricately linked relationships.

Estimating Age at Death

Generally speaking, the physical human body develops from conception until shortly after puberty, at which point the physical body maintains or degrades, as an individual continues to age chronologically (Halcrow and Tayles 2008). The development of the body follows a relatively predictable pattern that has been studied using osteological collections of individuals with known ages (Perry 2005; Lewis 2019). To estimate age at death, we examine patterns of biological age, that is, patterns of physical changes within the human body. With the application of established methods and standards, those physical manifestations of biological age are then translated to an estimated chronological age. However, as the development, and particularly the degradation, of the human body is still slightly variable, these age estimates are precisely that: estimates (Liversidge et al. 2015; O'Connell 2004). Consequently, age ranges or confidence intervals should be incorporated, demonstrating the uncertainty between biological and chronological age estimates. However, it should be noted that biological or chronological age estimates still do not equate to social age.

For non-adult remains, there are three main approaches to estimating biological age: dental development and eruption, long bone length, and epiphyseal fusion. When selecting a method, it is important to understand the reference collection used to establish or develop the methodology to help ensure comparability between the reference collection used to establish the method, and the sample under consideration, as age and growth can be mediated by ancestry, socio-economic status, nutritional status, and more. Other methods also exist to estimate age at death in non-adult remains, including measurements of the occipital (e.g., basilar part) and temporal bones. These are summarized in Schaefer *et al.* (2009).

Dental Development and Eruption

Perhaps the most reliable method to estimate age at death is dental development and eruption, as it is least likely to be affected by external factors (e.g., under nutrition) (White and Folkens 2012, 364; Brickley 2004). During their lifetime, humans have two sets of teeth: deciduous dentition (or, your baby teeth) and your permanent dentition (adult teeth). These teeth develop in conical structures from the crown of the tooth to the tip of the root. Deciduous teeth also resorb, that is, they start to disappear, starting from the roots, until the tooth falls out, making room for the permanent tooth to come up in its spot or crypt (Hillson 1996). The bone around the teeth is the alveolar bone, and it is constantly remodeling and adapting to the different teeth as they develop and erupt in the mouth (Figure 4).

When discussing dentition in humans, biological anthropologists divide the mouth into quadrants, and within each quadrant, we have a set number of

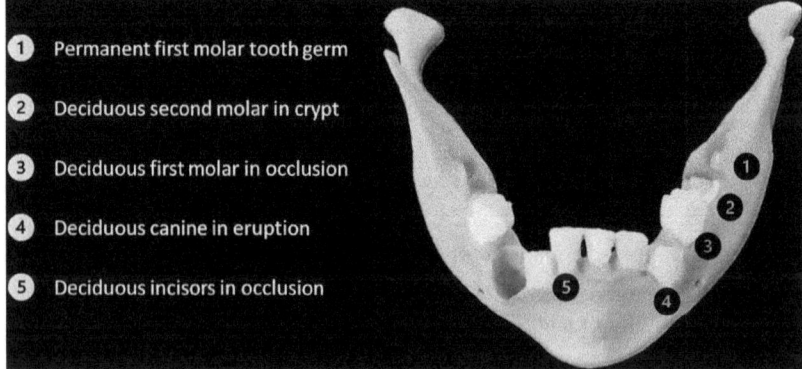

Figure 4 Non-adult mandible with deciduous teeth in occlusion, in eruption, and in alveolus (crypt). Photo by the author.

incisors, canines, premolars, and molars. In our deciduous dentition, each quadrant has two incisors, one canine, and two molars, for a dental formula of 2.1.0.2. In our adult dentition, each quadrant has two incisors, one canine, two premolars, and three molars, for a dental formula of 2.1.2.3. Each type of tooth has a specific use, from tearing and ripping into tough foods (like meat) to grinding and chewing fibrous foods (like plant materials).

To estimate an individuals age at death, we examine the development and eruption of each tooth or the entire dentition, observing how much of the tooth is present (e.g., just the crown, roots partly complete, roots are fully developed), and whether that tooth has erupted out of the bone (into occlusion) or it is still sitting in the alveolar bone. There are generally two approaches to consider dental development and eruption. The first is looking at a developmental chart that captures "ideal" development at particular ages (e.g., Ubelaker 1989). Then, you simply compare the dentition you are looking at to the images and find the one that most closely corresponds to it, or what two images the individual might be between, in order to get an estimated age range. The second is a little more complex. Instead of looking at the entire dentition as one item, you examine each tooth individually and come up with a very specific age range for the individual you are looking at (e.g., Gustafson and Koch 1974; Moorrees *et al.* 1963). It is a much more complex and time-consuming process, but the results are more specific to each individual rather than just a broad comparison. Alternatively, AlQahanti and colleagues (2010) have also developed an interactive software based on their London Tooth Atlas, whereby individuals examine dental development, compare dentition, and input dental development data and are provided an age estimate (Audsley & Khan 2024).

Dental development is considered most appropriate for individuals less than 16 years of age. For individuals older than this, age estimation relies heavily on the mineralization and eruption of the third molars (colloquially known as the wisdom teeth), which is subject to a great deal of variation, and consequently, may not provide a confident age estimation (White and Folkens, 2005).

Long Bone Length

Bioarchaeologists can also evaluate the length of unfused and complete long bones (i.e., arms and legs) to estimate age at death in non-adult remains. As discussed in Section 1, initial studies exploring infant and child remains were particularly interested in rates of growth during childhood. These studies concluded that growth follows a fairly predictable pattern in non-adult skeletal remains (Maresh 1970). Based on these findings, researchers subsequently established standards of long bone lengths based on chronological age (e.g.,

Maresh 1970). To estimate age at death based on long bone lengths, researchers measure a *complete* and *unfused* bone using an osteometric board, or calipers for smaller bones, and compare it to the charts provided to determine an age estimate. If an osteometric board is not available, a simple version can be easily made for in-field use, using graph paper (or a metric tape measurer), a flat surface, and two objects with thick flat ends (e.g., textbooks).

As the linear growth of an individual can be drastically influenced by internal and external factors (e.g., genetics, poor nutrition), it is important to consider that this approach is not as reliable or exact as other methods to estimate age at death (White and Folkens, 2005). For example, if someone experiences food insecurity and does not obtain proper nutrition while growing, their stature can become stunted (e.g., Mahfouz *et al.* 2021). Opportunities for "catch-up growth" exist, but acute or chronic stunting may occur. As a result, in communities where individuals experienced periods of nutritional stress, age estimates for non-adult skeletal remains may inadvertently be underestimated, that is, they may appear younger than they were at the time of death, due to acute or chronic stunting. However, White and Folkens (2005, p. 373) suggest that, in the absence of teeth or epiphyses, long bone length can be used to estimate the age of subadults. Consequently, this method should be applied with caution, or an understanding of the limitations, but is nevertheless a simple and effective way to estimate age in non-adult remains.

Epiphyseal Fusion

Researchers can also explore patterns of epiphyseal fusion, or the fusion of the growth plates at the ends of bones, to estimate age at death. Consider the humerus (Figure 5). In an adult, it is one solid bone; however, for non-adult remains, the bone comprises multiple pieces, including the diaphysis or shaft of the bone, and epiphyses or caps. As the individual ages, the bones continue to grow along the growth plate at the end of the shaft. Ossification and bone growth stops when the cells at the growth plate stop dividing and the epiphysis fuses to the end of the long bone.

Fusion of epiphyses occurs in known and predictable patterns, with slight variations depending on the individual, their biological sex, and the population (White and Folkens, 2005). Most epiphyseal activity occurs between the ages of 11 and 23, making this an ideal method for conducting age estimation on adolescent remains (White and Folkens, 2012). Additionally, White and Folkens (2012, 373) note that epiphyseal fusion and dental development are complementary aging techniques, as the methods slightly overlap and are often congruent with one another.

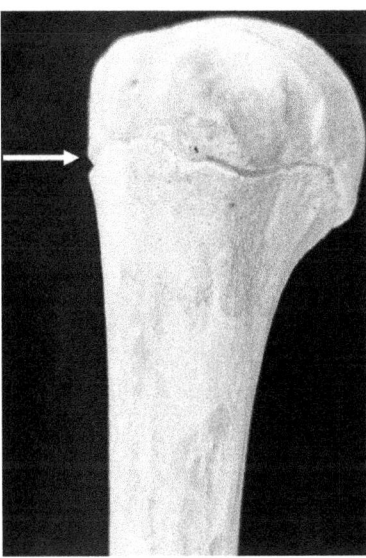

Figure 5 Right proximal humerus with the proximal epiphyseal fusion line still visible (indicated by arrow). Photo by the author.

Numerous age estimation methods using epiphyseal fusion have been established and used within bioarchaeology. Perhaps the most complete and comprehensive review of epiphyseal fusion and the appearance of secondary ossification centres is summarized by Scheuer and Black (2000) (updated by Cunningham *et al.*, 2016), but numerous methods have been applied based on epiphyseal fusion, consulting various reference collections (e.g., Hodges 1933; Greulich and Pyle 1950; Tanner *et al.*, 1983; Cardoso 2008a, 2008b). Many of these methods were developed using radiographic images and may not be entirely appropriate for macroscopic examination. Alternatively, the methods developed by Cardoso (2008a, 2008b) were developed using dry-bone observations, and are perhaps more appropriate for analysis of skeletal remains. In almost all approaches, however, bones are scored as unfused, fusing, or fused and compared to charts based on the bone and biological sex (if known/estimated), to estimate age at death. However, as indicated earlier, understanding the reference collection is necessary, as epiphyseal fusion timing can be influenced by a variety of factors, most significantly, socioeconomic status of a given population (Schmeling *et al.*, 2000, 2006).

Social Age

As previously discussed, social age corresponds to the culturally constructed perspectives of appropriate behaviours and responsibilities within a community.

As social age is not always directly related to the biology of our bodies, it can be difficult to ascertain bioarchaeologically. Why then, do we even need to consider social age? Consider a 12-year-old boy (Figure 6).

In the Anglo-Saxon period (England, 450–1066 CE), this individual might be married or serving in the military. In the medieval period (Europe, 1200–1700 CE) a 12-year-old boy might be an apprentice, learning a new skill and taking on new roles and responsibilities in their community. Today, however, a 12-year-old would likely be in school and starting a first job like a paper route or babysitting. Clearly, these individuals would have had different lived experiences, different expectations, and different risks. Treating these 12-year-olds as the same would be a gross oversimplification, and possibly contribute to inaccurate and misguided interpretations about their bodies and lives.

To understand social ages as they were practiced in the past, we might be able to look to historical or ancient literary sources that provide a guide to the life course models in the past. In other situations, however, we have to look at the bioarchaeological data to help us define the social age categories. Researchers are continuing to develop ways to assess social age in past populations, and it is important to note that the methods employed need to be appropriate to that community, and how social age may have been experienced or manifested at the archaeological and bioarchaeological levels.

In studying social age changes in the Romano-British period (1st–5th centuries CE), Rebecca Gowland (2006) examines mortuary profiles by looking at grave good distributions, working to understand changes in grave goods in relation to changes in social ages. Changes in grave good assemblages for females between the ages of 18 and 24 years may suggest the period in which young girls were married and became wives, mothers, or individuals running a household (Gowland 2006).

In the Roman period Gaul (4th–6th centuries CE), Avery and colleagues (2021) explore changes in diet, using dietary stable isotopes, finding marked changes for males around 16.5 years of age. Incorporating archaeological and ancient literary evidence, they suggest that this change is related to the social age transition to adolescence for young men as they began apprenticeships or began military service (Avery *et al.,* 2021).

Identifying ways in which social age may have been expressed and finding ways to explore these changes need to be considered on a site-by-site basis, incorporating other cross-cutting variables of identity including sex, gender, socio-economic status, immigration status, and more.

Figure 6 Approximation of a 12-year-old boy in the Anglo-Saxon, early medieval, and modern periods, as interpreted by AI. Images generated by the author.

The Process of Aging

While age is a fundamental aspect of bioarchaeological studies, biological anthropologists' engagement with age often takes a linear approach. First, researchers transform biological age (e.g., long bone length in non-adults) to chronological age estimates, using established osteological age estimation. However, we know that these methods are influenced by inter- and intra-population variation (Lewis 2019). To account for this variation, researchers then employ age categories (e.g., 0–5 years). In turn, these age categories are likened to a social age category (e.g., infancy), without recognizing the social constructionism of these age categories and how they may vary depending on the sex, status, and community of the individual (Inglis & Halcrow 2018). As Soafer (2011) highlights, this linear approach to the tripartite model not only inappropriately equates the three measures of age but turns the process of aging into a series of distinct categories, removing the fluidity and variability of aging within a community.

Due to the precise nature in which biological anthropologists can estimate age at death in infants and children, we have the unique opportunity to assess the process of aging, viewing age as a continuous, rather than categorical, variable. Researchers should be critical within their studies and determine if categorical variables are necessary to their analysis, rather than replicating standard approaches commonly used when analysing adult remains. While there may be limitations in the bioarchaeological study of infants and children, there are certainly exciting prospects and opportunities that need to be seized and expanded moving forward.

4 Sex and Gender

In anthropology and beyond, sex and gender are not synonymous but relate to two separate concepts (White and Folkens 2005, 385). Sex refers to the biological construct related to differences in chromosomes, genitalia, and secondary sexual characteristics (Fausto-Sterling *et al.*, 2012). When discussing biological sex, researchers use the terms male, female, and intersex. Within biological anthropology, there are a number of established methods used to estimate biological sex, with varying degrees of certainty or success (see the following subsection).

Gender, however, is a social or cultural construct that relates to how we are treated, and how we should, or choose to, behave and act within our communities (Zuckerman & Crandall 2019). When discussing gender, researchers use the terminology man, woman, non-binary, and other culturally specific terms (e.g., two-spirited in some Native American or Indigenous communities in North

America). There are a lot of ways to "get at" gender (see Hollimon 2011, and Hollimon 2017), but as gender is a social construct, the ways in which gender is perceived and expressed can differ in each social group, so these approaches are used with varying degrees of success. Similar to investigations of social age, each needs to be investigated within their own cultural context, ideally with the application of feminist or queer theoretical frameworks to support interpretations (see Agarwal & Wesp 2017, Geller 2008).

Estimating Biological Sex

Although almost all parts of the human skeleton exhibit some degree of variation between biological sexes, sex estimation of adult skeletal remains traditionally focuses on features of the pelvis and cranium, where dimorphic features are most pronounced (White and Folkens 2005). Generally, these differences are described as *sexual dimorphism*, that is, the differences in physical characteristics or physiology between two dominantly defined sex-based groups (typically, male versus female). The challenge with this language is that it presents the expression of biological sex in a dichotomous pair rather than as within a spectrum, misrepresenting the variety of expressions within the human (and non-human) species (Wesp 2017). Despite bioarchaeologists arguing since the 1990s that biological sex does not operate within a binary, the language of sexual dimorphism and use of male/female dichotomies persists (Hollimon 2017, 51).

When estimating morphological biological sex from skeletal remains, bioarchaeologists prefer to use features of the pelvis and cranium. That is, looking at the shape and form of the pelvis and cranium for features that exhibit a range of sex-linked manifestations. When pelvic and cranial methods are used in tandem, these approaches can produce the most reliable biological sex estimations from morphological assessments. However, the features examined in these methods develop during the later stage of puberty, meaning they are appropriate for post-pubertal skeletal remains, as well as peri-pubertal remains, with lower degrees of accuracy (Sanchez and Hoppa 2022). They are not, however, reliable for pre-pubertal skeletal remains.

Non-adult sex estimation methods also exist but are generally less reliable than adult specific methods. In fact, Mary Lewis (2007) calls a reliable non-adult sex estimation method the "holy grail" within biological anthropology: something that has not yet been found but is highly coveted. The intention behind establishing a reliable method to estimate biological sex is not simply to further categorize humans, but rather, that biological sex may offer an important lens to understanding lived experiences in the past. For example, if boys and girls were treated very differently, incorporating biological sex estimations to help us understand the consequences of these different patterns of treatment can provide insights into long-term consequences, or health status within past populations. For example, in Colombia (1000–1400 CE), Miller and colleagues (2018) found that sex-specific patterns of food consumption did not emerge later in life, but were present during childhood as well.

The common adult and non-adult methods are outlined in what follows, as well as biochemical and metric approaches that can be applied to all ages. While these methods exist, it is important to note that no morphological method for assessing biological sex in non-adult skeletal remains is considered "acceptable" by most osteologists (Buikstra and Ubelaker 1994, 16).

Biological Sex in Adult Remains

Sex estimation in fully mature skeletal remains is most commonly estimated using features of the pelvis and cranium, following methods summarized by Buikstra and Ubelaker (1994). Pelvic dimorphism is estimated after examining five features: ventral arc, subpubic concavity, ischiopubic ramus ridge, greater sciatic notch, and preauricular sulcus (Klales *et al.*, 2012; Kenyhercz *et al.*, 2017). Cranial dimorphism is based largely on robusticity, size, and shape, and is assessed using five morphological features: nuchal crest, mastoid process, supraorbital margin, glabella, and mental eminence (Buikstra and Ubelaker 1994). After analysis of these features, the individual is assigned to one of six categories, following Buikstra and Ubelaker (1994), including male, probable male, ambiguous, probable female, female, and undetermined. In instances where the pelvic and cranial morphologies are not in agreement, greater emphasis should be given to pelvic dimorphism, as this is considered the most dimorphic skeletal aspect and most reliable method for estimating sex in adult skeletal remains (White and Folkens 2005). Similar to age estimates or other methodological approaches, researchers should consider the reference sample on which they are developed in order to determine the most appropriate method based on the population under study. Furthermore, while these methods are widely established and utilized within the field of bioarchaeology, it is important to note their limitations in capturing the full range of variation seen in expressions of biological sex, particularly in their exclusion of intersex individuals (Wesp 2017).

Biological Sex in Non-adult Remains

To estimate biological sex in non-adults (i.e., pre-pubertal remains), researchers have tried to develop other methods, but with little success. In fact, even for an experienced researcher using non-adult sex estimation methods, sex estimations likely only have a 70 per cent accuracy, particularly for children over the age of 10 (Lewis 2019).

For the non-adult specific methods, there are three approaches, including the non-adult mandible (Schutkowski 1993), the unfused ilia (Schutkowski 1993; Sutter 2003), and the fused distal humerus (Rogers 1999, 2009). Rather than scoring features on a five-point scale commonly used in adult sex estimation methods, non-adult sex estimation methods simply rely on male/female dichotomies (Schutkowski 1993; Sutter 2003). However, some researchers examining biological sex in non-adult remains prefer to use the terminology "probable male" and "probable female" in order to further indicate the uncertainty using these methods (e.g., Arthur *et al.* 2016). The methods have demonstrated sex-based biases (e.g., non-adult mandible more reliably estimated biological males than biological females; Schutkowski 1993), and age-related dependencies (e.g., unfused iliac may work best on individuals aged 6 to 15 (Sutter 2003)). More recently, Vlak *et al.* (2008) found that methods associated with the unfused ilia failed to predict sex accurately, suggesting further work is needed to understand the ontogeny of sexual dimorphism, particularly within non-adult remains.

Dental Metrics

One problem with established methods is that they tend to be sample specific. However, when the method is applied to a different sample, the accuracy rate tends to be lower than in the original study (Buikstra and Ubelaker 1994; Cardoso 2008c; Vlak *et al.* 2008). To overcome this limitation, researchers advocate for site-specific methods, where factors such as nutrition, living conditions, and even genetic variation may be better mediated (Cardoso 2008c).

One approach that overcomes this limitation is site-specific dental metrics (Cardoso 2008c). The use of dental metrics has been acknowledged as a viable method of sex estimation, particularly in the mandibular canines, which show the greatest degree of sexual dimorphism (Hillson 1996). In the approach outlined by Cardoso (2008c), permanent teeth are measured in the mesodistal (MD) and faciolingual (FL) or buccal-lingual (BL) planes, to the nearest tenth of a millimeter (Figure 7). Any tooth selected should be unobscured by dental wear or carious lesions, to ensure a full and complete measurement is taken.

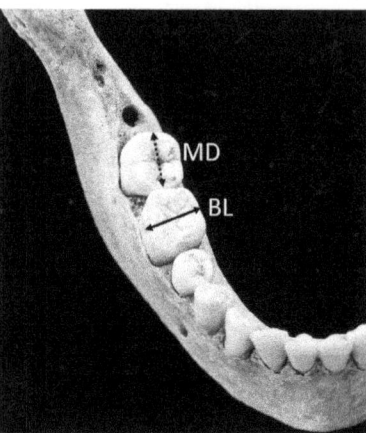

Figure 7 Directions of tooth measurements indicated, including buccal-lingual (or labial lingual) (solid arrow) and mesio-distal (dotted arrow). Photo by the author.

For each measurement (i.e., FL, MD) of each tooth, the sample mean is calculated, which serves as the sectioning point for the entire unidentified sample. Any individual with a measurement greater than the sectioning point is estimated male, while any individual with a measurement less than the sectioning point is estimated female. Where the sex-ratio is known to be imbalanced (e.g., cemetery associated with a military fort occupied predominantly by men), this approach will not be appropriate.

Beyond its site specificity, the main strength of this approach is that it does not require a comparative sample of adult remains nor a comparative subsample of known-sex individuals. Furthermore, the sectioning point procedure can be applied to poorly preserved samples and non-adult remains, so long as permanent dentition is present (Cardoso 2008c). The approach is not applicable to deciduous dentition.

In using this approach, Cardoso (2008c) found that the canine was consistently the most sexually dimorphic, with an accuracy of more than 80 per cent, and was less affected by small sample sizes than other teeth in the dentition. Premolars also had high accuracy compared to other teeth (Cardoso 2008c). In instances where the canine or premolar measurements disagree with one another, greater emphasis should be given to the canine, as this is the more dimorphic element of the dentition (Hillson 1996).

To help assess if dental metric measurements are performed reliably, intraobserver error measurements should also be taken (e.g., intraclass correlation coefficients). Measurements with a strong correlation between the first and second measurements can be considered reliable and used to estimate sex for individuals with permanent dentition present.

Ancient DNA and Peptide Analysis

While multiple morphological methods exist to estimate biological sex in non-adult remains, the accuracy rates of these methods are between 60 and 85 per cent (depending on the method used, the sample consulted, or the sex of the individual) (Falys *et al.* 2005; Buikstra and Ubelaker 1994). Clearly, significant challenges and limitations exist. To estimate biological sex more accurately than morphological methods allow, biological anthropologists have turned to biomolecular approaches, using ancient DNA (aDNA) and peptide analysis.

Ancient DNA analysis of biological sex can be accomplished through polymerase chain reaction (PCR) amplification of the sex-chromosome-linked amelogenin alleles (e.g., Tierney & Bird 2015), or through Shot-Gun Sequencing and considering the ratio of sequences that align to X and Y chromosomes (e.g., Skoglund *et al.* 2013). For example, Mays (2001) utilized aDNA of infant remains, to explore sex-specific patterns of infanticide in Roman Britain.

Peptide analysis focuses on the isolation and examination of sex-linked peptides of amelogenin in dental enamel (Stewart *et al.* 2016, 2017; Parker *et al.* 2019). Minimally destructive in nature, this method is more cost effective, and less prone to contamination than aDNA (Stewart *et al.*, 2016, Buonasera *et al.* 2020). Furthermore, the applicability of the method to both permanent and deciduous dentition, as well as dental germs, makes it a new avenue for researchers interested in non-adult sex estimation methods (Gowland *et al.* 2021). For example, Avery *et al.* (2022) applied peptide analysis to the analysis of adolescent remains in order to explore sex-specific patterns of pubertal timing, while Lugli *et al.* (2020) incorporated peptide analysis to explore sex-specific patterns of morbidity and mortality in non-adults.

While these biomolecular approaches have the capability to produce more reliable sex estimations than morphological assessment, there are two significant limitations. The first is the cost: while morphological methods can be completed in the field with limited or no equipment, aDNA and peptide analysis require specialized training, equipment, and laboratory spaces. Secondly, and more importantly, is the ethical considerations of performing destructive analysis on human remains. In some contexts, this will not be a limiting factor, but in other contexts, particularly when working with Indigenous ancestral remains, destructive methods are not supported. In these instances, researchers are required to rely on morphological assessments, or not consider biological sex in their analyses, of non-adult remains.

Exploring Gender

As discussed at the start of this section, sex and gender refer to two different constructs: the biological, and the social. While bioarchaeological methods have been developed to assess biological sex, assessment of gender is much more challenging. Some researchers work to assess gender independently of biological sex and incorporate other methods with varying degrees of success. Much like investigations into social age, the methods and approaches used to assess gender need to be site specific and relevant to the community or sample under study. For example, while grave goods may be used in some contexts to suggest gendered identities, implicating weaponry as a "masculine" item may be highly inappropriate in contexts where more than just men contributed to fighting. To date, very little research has considered gender in children, which offers an exciting area of development for future researchers: to consider how we might investigate gendered experiences in the past, and how gender may have shaped the lives of children and their communities by extension.

One avenue that offers promising results to explore gendered experiences of childhood is the sex-specific analysis of diet. By studying teeth that developed during childhood, but were archaeologically recovered from adult remains, researchers can employ more reliable sex estimation methods (e.g., pelvic and cranial dimorphism), and investigate experiences of childhood trapped in adult remains. Through the contextual analysis of the results, we can begin to understand how males and females were treated or behaved within their communities, thus offering insights into gendered patterns of behaviour.

For example, Miller and colleagues (2020) use stable isotope analysis of incremental dentine segments to explore sex-specific patterns of breastfeeding, weaning, and childhood diets, in Eastern Zhou period (771–221 BCE) China. Through this gendered exploration of diet, they find that dietary differences between sex-specific groups emerged during childhood, suggesting a cultural gendering of individuals in ancient China (Miller *et al.,* 2020). Using a similar methodology, Avery and colleagues (2021) explore sex-based patterns of dietary change in Roman Imperial adolescence. By exploring changes in diet along with archaeological and literary evidence, Avery *et al.* (2021) propose that the changing patterns correspond to changing social age roles that were different for males and females, suggesting that gender-based patterns of social age change as individuals reach the period of adolescence. In using this approach, we are once again reminded of how aspects of our identities (age, sex/gender, ethnicity, etc.) overlap and intersect with one another to produce our own individual lived experiences.

5 Growth Disruptions

Through clinical and biomedical research, we know a lot about human bone growth and development. Generally, postnatal growth in humans occurs most rapidly between birth and approximately three years of age (Sanders *et al.* 2017). Between approximately three years of age and the onset of puberty, the childhood growth phase includes a slower, but steady, height increase (Sanders *et al.* 2017). The onset of puberty corresponds with the beginning of the adolescent growth spurt, during which individuals grow between 7 and 10 centimetres per year (Sadler 2017). Shortly after puberty, the bones fuse and adult stature is largely achieved. At this point, any additional change in height is predominantly related to soft tissue changes, such as the amount of space between your vertebrae, although some ossification continues (e.g., vertebrae annual rings).

The description above is only a broad generalization, and individual rates of growth vary depending on age and sex, as well as between and within populations. Some of that population variation is controlled by genetics, but environmental factors can also play a significant role (Bogin 1999, Goodman and Armelagos 1989). This means that while your entire height and growth potential are linked to your genetics, there are a lot of factors that influence whether you can make it to that full height potential or not. Factors like altitude, climate, exposure to toxins, and psychological stress can all influence growth, but the two factors that play the largest role are nutrition and disease.

Nutritionally, individuals that do not get enough food or enough nutrients in their diet will have slowed or delayed growth, which may result in stunted stature. Pathologically, some diseases are known to cause stunting, like rickets, whereas other diseases or illnesses may not directly cause the growth delay, but various symptoms of the disease can. For example, you might not have the same appetite to eat when you are sick, so you may not get the same nutrients, or you might experience vomiting and diarrhea, meaning, even if you are still eating, your body is unable to uptake nutrients the same way.

While we have a good idea of the general conditions that contribute to growth and development, thanks to more than 50 years of research in this area, we are still unable to tease apart which factor is responsible for altering growth and development in any one population or any one person. That means, instead of looking at growth and development to talk specifically about the impact of a particular disease or nutritional deficiency, we use growth and development as a broad measure of population health. Or, more specifically, we use *disruptions* to growth and development as a proxy for *poor* health (Goodman and Armelagos 1989; Halcrow and Tayles 2008). Effectively, those with poor growth likely experienced poorer nutrition and/or heavier disease burden that those with normal growth patterns. If an entire population indicates growth stunting, it may suggest broad patterns of nutritional or disease burden within the community.

The terms growth and development refer to two different patterns of maturation. Growth refers to increase in size or mass, while development is the progression of changes from an immature state to a mature state. When considering age estimation methods, for example, long bone length is a measure of growth, because the bones are increasing in size; while epiphyseal fusion is a measure of development, as the size of the bones are not of importance, but the changes in the fusion of the growth plates are.

To examine these patterns of growth and development, biological anthropologists look at pre-pubertal non-adults, because they have immature immune systems and very rapid rates of growth, meaning that they are the most sensitive to environmental disruptions (Lewis 2007). In contrast, peri-pubertal individuals tend to have the most robust immune systems, meaning more minor infections or diseases might not result in any growth changes (Lewis 2022), and adults have already finished growing, so assessing patterns of growth and development would be futile. Analysis of adults, however, can be useful to consider full height achieved within an individual, sample, or population.

By assessing patterns of growth and development, or disruptions to growth and development, we can learn about political, economic, or social circumstances, or about the impact of subsistence changes (e.g., Dhavale *et al.* 2017).

Methodological Approaches

To investigate patterns of growth and development, there are five key methodological approaches: long bone lengths, cortical thickness, body mass, enamel hypoplastic defects, and vertebral neural canal shape and size.

Long Bone Lengths (Endochondral Growth)

One of the main ways that bones grow is in length, what we call endochondral growth. In this process, new bone develops at the ends of the diaphysis or shaft of the bone, beneath the growth plate, increasing the overall length of the bone (Mays 2018). For studies of growth, an assessment of long bone length is the most common approach and is a long-accepted method for assessing general health and stress in a population (Ruff *et al.* 2013). There are a few reasons why this approach is so commonly applied. First, long bones tend to survive well within the archaeological record, which means bioarchaeologists are able to incorporate large sample sizes and create robust datasets. Additionally, because long bones are big (compared to other bones), any small change can be more easily seen or detected than in smaller elements, allowing us to pick up on smaller perturbations or changes in growth. Lastly, with the use of various equations, we can also estimate stature to compare to modern samples more easily than only looking at the length of specific bones.

In this method, *complete* and *unfused* diaphyses are measured, using calipers or an osteometric board, depending on resources available and the length of the bone. Measurements should be taken following standard methods by Buikstra and Ubelaker (1994) to ensure comparability between studies.

Once data is collected, comparisons of raw data are made to appropriate standards. You should incorporate appropriate standards relevant to your particular sample, but common reference standards include the Maresh reference data, established from a sample of healthy middle-class children from Denver, Colorado (Maresh 1943, 1955, 1970), or the World Health Organization (WHO) international child growth standard (WHO Multicentre Growth Reference Study Group, 2006a, 2006b).

For example, in a study of infants and children from prehistoric Ban Non Wat (Northeast Thailand), Dhavale and colleagues (2017) assessed the impacts that result from the adoption of agriculture. In their study, Dhavale *et al.* (2017) found no difference in linear growth patterns between chronological phases, suggesting that the transition to intensified agricultural practices may have provided a buffer from biological stress that is not commonly observed in other parts of the world.

Cortical Thickness (Appositional Growth)

Just like bones can grow in length, bones also grow in thickness, what we call appositional growth, with the shaft of the bone increasing in width. Specifically, bone is deposited beneath the periosteum on the outer surface of the diaphysis (Mays 2018). As new bone is forming on the outer surface, bone on the inner surface or endosteal surface is resorbed, altering the size of the internal medullary cavity. Generally, the rate of subperiosteal apposition outpaces endosteal resorption, increasing the bone width and the cortical thickness (i.e., thickness of the walls surrounding the marrow cavity) (Mays 2018). While long bone length tracks growth relative to stature, cortical thickness is more closely related to growth in body mass (Ruff *et al.* 2013). As such, the two processes (endochondral growth and appositional growth) are often investigated in tandem, to provide a more thorough understanding of growth and development in past populations (e.g., Dhavale *et al.* 2017).

By measuring the thickness of the bone from the medullary cavity to the outside surface, we can measure the cortical thickness of the bone. In a normal, healthy individual, appositional growth occurs at a faster pace than resorption during subadult growth. This means that, in normal growth, cortical thickness should increase during non-adult development. However, when malnourished, clinical studies have demonstrated that rates of endosteal resorption increase, resulting in reduced cortical thickness for age, or a thinner bone (Mays 2018). In past populations, cortical thickness-for-age is generally less comparable to modern populations, indicating that past populations experienced more nutritional stress than we do today. Furthermore, increased activity levels in prepubertal children may result in increased deposition along the subperiosteal surface; as a result, researchers may be able to differentiate between nutritional and biomechanical factors that contribute to altered cortical thickness (Mays 2018).

To measure cortical thickness, we use radiographs or x-rays, and measure at the mid-point of the shaft of particular bones. Specifically, you measure the total subperiosteal width (T) and the medullary width (M). By subtracting the medullary width from the total subperiosteal width, you get the cortical thickness (Equation 1 and Figure 8). Cortical indices (CI) can then be calculated to help standardize the cortical volume for bone size, allowing researchers to evaluate changes in apposition growth in relation to age.

$$CI = (T–M)/T * 100 \qquad (1)$$

Equation 1 Cortical index calculation

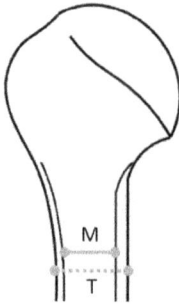

Figure 8 Illustration demonstrating difference between medullary cavity (M) and total subperiosteal thickness (T), used to calculate cortical thickness. Illustration by the author.

There has been a recent push to use CT scans instead of X-rays, which are higher resolution, and allow for a more subtle measurement of differences, but getting access to this type of equipment might be hard to do in the field, so it may not be appropriate in all cases.

Generally, the acquisition of cortical bone is a more sensitive index of environmental stress than long bone length (Mays 2018). Thus, regardless of using x-rays or CT scans, investigating cortical thicknesses is considered a more sensitive indicator of poor conditions during the growth period. The only trade-off is that you need more specialized equipment to take the measurements than measuring linear growth.

Body Mass

Measurements of body mass are also routinely used to assess health in a population, as improved nutrition and living conditions have been shown to result in greater weight and stature in non-adults. While numerous studies explore body mass calculations for adults, there are significantly fewer studies focused on non-adult remains (Ruff *et al.* 2013). This can be problematic, as growth and development are largely influenced by genetics. Thus, using a comparable population is essential for identifying accurate assessment of body mass.

To calculate body mass in non-adults, measurements of the femur can be applied to age-specific equations (Ruff 2007). For this approach you can use an osteometric board or sliding calipers for assessments of dry bones or take measurements from x-rays and radiographs, with measurements taken to the nearest millimetre.

Linear Enamel Hypoplasia

Hypoplastic defects are the result of episodic growth disruptions captured in dental enamel during permanent and, to a lesser degree, deciduous tooth crown formation (Hillson 2014; Lewis 2007). Defects can manifest as furrow-type defects, pit-type defects, plane-type defects (large areas of brown stria planes), or localized hypoplasia of primary canines (LHPC) (Hillson 2008, 166–167; Lukacs 2009).

As your teeth are forming, the crown develops from the crown to the root. During this process, ameloblasts, the cells responsible for developing the enamel prior to mineralization are very sensitive to disruptions and do not work properly when they are under stress (Temple 2020; Lewis 2007). This can be nutritional stress or pathological stress, but it can even be impacted by psychosocial stress (see Kinaston *et al.*, 2019; Marini & Flensborg 2023). In these instances of prolonged increased stress, the enamel is affected. These defects can show up in the form of bands across the tooth that almost look like someone has put a really tight elastic band around it or pitting in an area where the enamel is just missing (or, very thin) (Figure 9). These marks are called hypoplastic defects, while the overall condition is called enamel hypoplasia.

Hypoplastic defects are generally non-specific indicators of stress during the growth period, meaning that the specific cause of growth disruption cannot be identified (Mays 2018, 80). However, compared to linear or appositional growth, these dental defects represent periods of stress that were survived by the individual, meaning we are not entirely reliant on individuals who died during stressful periods to observe these defects.

A key benefit of exploring hypoplastic defects is that they are often visible to the naked eye or accessible by imaging techniques, meaning that x-rays, CT scans, or other potentially expensive equipment are not necessary to evaluate the condition. Due to the known development patterns of teeth, it is also possible to track where the hypoplastic defect is on the tooth and trace it back to the age at which the individual experienced developmental stress (Reid & Dean 2006). For example, studying 18th- and 19th-century populations in

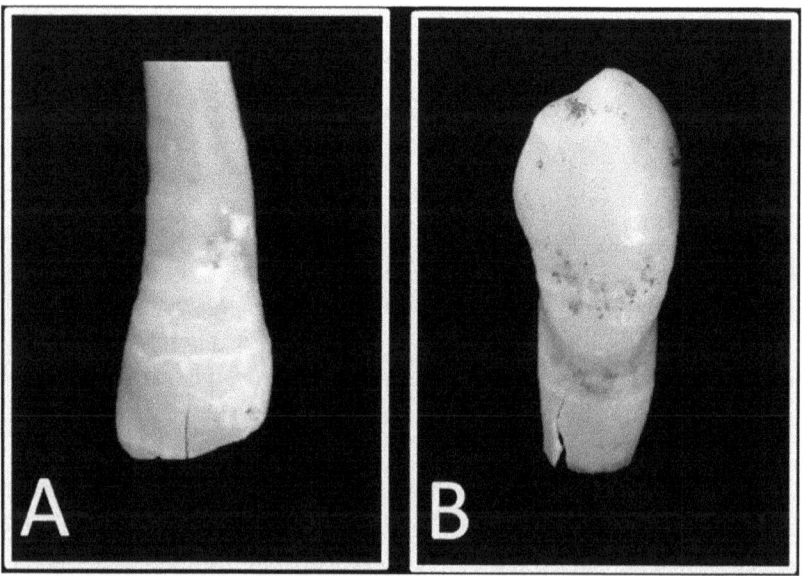

Figure 9 Enamel hypoplastic defects including (A) linear defects and (B) linear defects and pitting. Dental samples from Apollonia, Greece. Photos by the author.

Japan, Nakayama (2016) concluded that the frequency and timing of hypoplastic defects occurred between two and four years of age, which they suggest may be related to weaning stress (i.e., following the introduction of complementary foods or after the cessation of breastfeeding). Similarly, in a study of linear enamel hypoplastic defects (LEHs) in Late/Final Jamon period hunter-gatherers (Japan), Temple (2020) found that the majority of LEHs were identified between 2.0 and 4.0 years of age, corresponding to a period of social age transition, partly mediated by the cessation of breastfeeding. However, Temple (2020, 74) also acknowledges that the organization of enamel in the occlusal region of the tooth versus that in the cervical region of the tooth are different, which may contribute to the more weakly defined LEHs in the occlusal region of the teeth. Thus, it is important to consider both internal and external interpretations of growth disruption in the human body.

Vertebral Neural Canals

The use of dimensions of non-adult vertebral neural canal (VNC) and vertebral bodies can also be used as an indicator of growth disruption (Newman & Gowland 2015; Amoroso & Garcia 2018). Research has demonstrated that reduced vertebral canal size has been linked with stunted growth development, and decreased health (Clark *et al.*, 1986; Watts 2011). Particularly exciting with this approach is that, while growth disruptions captured in long bone lengths may become distorted by effects of catch-up growth, VNC captures early postnatal growth disruptions that become "locked in" and cannot be remodeled during later growth and development (Newman and Gowland 2015, 156; Lewis 2019).

The vertebrae form in three ossification centres: the vertebral body, the left neural arch, and the right neural arch (Cunningham *et al.,* 2016). The vertebral neural canal (VNC) then surrounds the spinal cord and is positioned within the vertebral foramen. To assess VNC measurements, researchers rely on multiple measurements. First is the vertebral body height, which increases rapidly during birth to five years of age and during the pubertal growth spurt, with a period of reduced growth rate between these periods (Newman and Gowland 2015). The majority of the neural arch growth, however, is completed relatively early within the postnatal growth period, with the left and right neural arch fuses along the spinous process around 1.5 years of age, and the neural arches fuses to the vertebral body by five years of age (Cunningham *et al.,* 2017).

Measurements of vertebral body height are taken from the midline of the centrum. As the vertebrae develop and fuse at different age points, this approach should be applied to vertebral bodies C3 to L5, where possible. Measurements of the VNC assess the transverse (TR) diameter of the neural canal (i.e., the

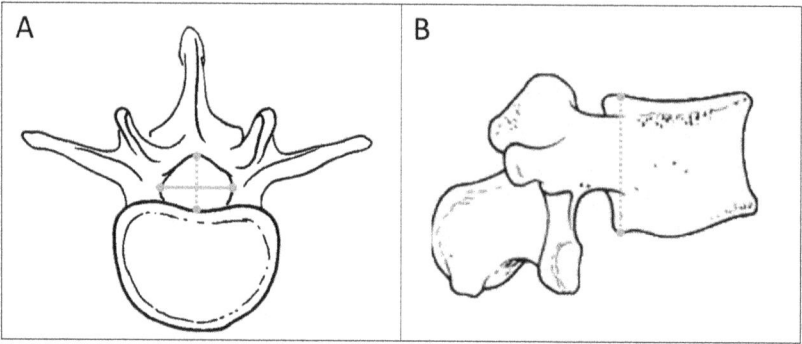

Figure 10 Vertebral neural canal measurements including (A) anterior-posterior (dotted line) and transverse (solid line), and (B) vertebral body height. Illustration by the author.

farthest distance between the medial surfaces of the pedicles) and anterior-posterior (AP) diameter (i.e., posterior surface of the vertebral body to the further opposite point of the neural canal) (Figure 10). The latter should only be applied when fusion of the neural arches and vertebral bodies has initiated. All measurements should be taken with sliding calipers to the nearest 0.01 mm.

In 2023, Brzobohatá and colleagues (2023) used VNC to assess stressful early-childhood experiences in a population associated with silver mining in medieval Czechia (13th–16th centuries CE). Incorporating TR, AP, and vertebral body height (BH) measurements, they found evidence of health stress events during early childhood, which contributed to early mortality in males. Females, however, appear to have been better buffered against these early-life stress events, raising questions about female life course experiences or biological differences in processing stress (Brzobohatá *et al.*, 2023).

Assumptions and Methodological Considerations

As with most of bioarchaeology, there are some common caveats to keep in mind when assessing growth and development.

The first is the issue of mortality bias. When looking at skeletons, we must keep in mind that we are looking at deceased individuals, or the non-survivors of the community (Wood *et al.* 1992). This is especially true of looking at non-adult remains. Said another way, when we examine non-adult remains and patterns of their growth and development, we are evaluating individuals that died as children. So, are their experiences really comparable or representative of non-adults that became adults? Can we say that the growth patterns of those who died are the same as the growth patterns of those who lived? Or did exposure to conditions that stunted their growth mirror conditions that contributed to their death? Would the survivors have experienced the same conditions that affected their growth and development? These questions may not have immediate answers, but can be explored in various ways, allowing us to investigate mortality bias (e.g., exploring enamel hypoplasia in non-adult remains and adult remains).

The second caveat is the issue or confounding factor of biological sex. Growth differs for males and females, especially around adolescence, due to hormones. But, as discussed in Section 4, biological sex estimation of non-adult remains is problematic, with no standard method that is generally accepted by osteologists. For many researchers, this means we must combine data for males and females into one sample, possibly blurring results and slight differences in various populations. With advancements in biomolecular approaches to biological sex estimation, there are possibilities of overcoming these issues, but not in a way that is currently accessible to all researchers and all studies.

6 Diet and Feeding

Eating is about a lot more than caloric intake. Rather, it is often related to what is available and appropriate to eat, whether due to economic, environmental, social, political, religious, or even personal reasons. As a result, by investigating diet we can start to learn about different choices made within a community. For example, do males eat more meat than females? What might that tell us about gender dynamics and social roles? Do lower-social-status individuals experience more nutritional stress compared to higher-status individuals? What might that tell us about economic availability, or structural biases and/or violence? Ultimately, what can diet tell us about food choices and food access within that population?

When we are applying these questions to adult remains, we can pick up broad and large-scale differences between groups. By investigating the diets of children using non-adult remains, however, we can start to understand the smaller differences, as children are more sensitive to dietary changes and nutritional stress within a community. We can also investigate child-specific practices, including infant feeding practices or weaning patterns, to learn about the differences in practices between various socioeconomic classes or cultural groups (Waters-Rist 2023). Childhood diet and the weaning processes also have important implications for early and later life health, mortality patterns, and fertility in past societies. So, much like growth and development studies, evidence concerning weaning and childhood diet can be used to provide insight into a community as a whole.

Diet and Weaning

Weaning is the extended process in which infants transition from receiving all nutrients from breastmilk to obtaining nutrients from sources other than breastmilk (weaning cessation). During this process, infants are introduced to complementary foods; that is, foods other than breastmilk that are brought in and used in tandem with breastmilk. Typically, breastmilk has everything to support a child up until six months. After this point, the breastmilk must be supplemented with other foods to ensure children are receiving all necessary nutrition to support growth and development.

In the past, weaning was a very dangerous period of a child's life. Weaning foods were often under-nutritious because they did not provide all the nutrients needed, or were even harmful, containing nutrients that the child is not yet able to metabolise. For example, while cow's milk can be consumed by much of the population without any detrimental factors, the consumption of cow's milk by infants can cause kidney failure and renal damage (Ziegler, 2007). As a result, consuming this type of food as a weaning food may contribute to malnutrition or even death in some instances. Conversely, human breastmilk contains a wide range of antibodies and probiotics, giving the infant immune support from the immune system of the individual providing the breastmilk. Once fully weaned, however, that infant must rely entirely on their own undeveloped immune system. As a result, a period of weaning – reducing intake of antibiotic-rich breast milk and increasing consumption of inadequate or dangerous foods – can be a dangerous, or even deadly, period in a child's life.

To explore patterns of diet and feeding in past populations, we may look to broad indicators of diet, including dental health, or more specific indicators, like dietary stable isotopes.

Dental Health

An analysis of dental health often includes an analysis of multiple dental health conditions, including rates of carious lesions (cavities) and dental wear, which can tell us a lot about diet. Cavities can be influenced by several factors, although diet is arguably the most important, and as such, the rate of carious lesions can tell us how cariogenic food may have been, which can tell us about carbohydrate or sugar intake (Hillson 1996, 2008). Meanwhile, dental wear can tell us how tough and abrasive food may have been. For non-adults more specifically, a wear pattern on the front baby teeth might be able to tell us if the infant was bottle fed (Scott & Halcrow 2017). Or the presence and rate of cavities could tell us about the type of food used for weaning. How old an individual is when those cavities and dental wear patterns start appearing might even tell us about the timing of weaning in a population, or if there was a sudden change in child diets (e.g., Prowse *et al.* 2008).

Dental Presence

To explore rates of carious lesions or dental wear, we must first have a record of what teeth are present and their overall condition. If we have an individual represented by one tooth, and it has a carious lesion, we might say that the individual has a 100 per cent caries rate, but this description may not be entirely representative of their entire dentition.

Teeth often are recorded as present or absent following Buikstra and Ubelaker (1994). If missing, the suspected timing (antemortem, post-mortem) should also be noted. Antemortem tooth loss (AMTL) can be distinguished from post-mortem tooth loss and congenitally absent teeth based on the degree of resorption of alveolar bone, and the presence or absence of wear facets on adjacent teeth, respectively.

Carious Lesions

Carious lesions should be recorded by tooth and location on the tooth, recording areas where clear demineralization had taken place, rather than areas of discolouration. Although this approach only captures later stages of cavities, and not 'pre-cavitated' lesions, it is the most common approach in bioarchaeology, allowing for comparisons to other published studies (Hillson 2001; Lukacs 2008).

Following Moore and Corbett (1971, 1973), carious lesions should be identified based on the tooth and tooth surface, including the occlusal surface, interproximal surface, lingual surface, cemento-enamel junction, or roots of the tooth. In instances where the carious lesions are too large to determine where they originated, they can defined as gross carious lesions.

There are multiple approaches to calculate caries rates, each with its own strengths and benefits. However, most studies use a caries rate by individual (Equation 2). Although this approach represents the observed caries frequency, rather than the real caries frequency, and does not take into consideration the impact of antemortem or post-mortem tooth loss, it is the most commonly employed method within bioarchaeology and allows for comparisons to other archaeological sites and samples.

$$Caries\ Rate = \frac{Number\ of\ carious\ teeth}{Number\ of\ observed\ teeth} \times 100 \qquad (2)$$

Equation 2 Caries rate by individual

Observation of caries rates by tooth type, location, or overall rate can help inform researchers about changes in diet, differences between samples or populations, and, with the use of theoretical frameworks, can help tell us about diet in the past.

Stable Isotopes

Beyond macroscopic analyses of dental structures, dietary stable isotope analysis offers a biochemical approach to better understand dietary intake and consumption. This is a destructive approach (i.e., a sample must be destroyed to obtain the associated data) but has been widely used within biological anthropology with applications to bones and teeth. A detailed review of dietary stable isotopes is beyond the scope of this Element, but a thorough introduction can be found in Katzenberg and Waters-Rist (2019).

Broadly, stable isotope analysis is based on the phrase "you are what you eat." As you eat food, your body uses the nutrients and minerals to form the tissues of your body. This means that, by examining the body (e.g., bones, teeth), we can work backwards to learn a bit about the foods you consumed. Now this approach does not produce a menu, listing every item an individual consumed as a child, but can tell us about the stable carbon and nitrogen values, from which bioarchaeologists can make inferences about the types of foods that individual consumed in life.

Particularly beneficial for studies of non-adults is the analysis of nitrogen isotopes, which is used to differentiate between trophic level of foods consumed. As we move up the food chain (e.g., plants to herbivores, to carnivores), nitrogen values should increase by approximately three to five per mil (Katzenberg & Waters-Rist 2019). In the case of infants, breastfeeding children should be approximately three per mil higher than the individual from which they are consuming breastmilk, as the infants are consuming their tissues and products (i.e., breastmilk). As it is often impossible to associate a deceased breastfeeding infant with the deceased individual from which they were breastfeeding, researchers use the average nitrogen values of adult females as the baseline (e.g., Richards *et al.* 2006). Infants that are then approximately three per mil higher than this proxy are assumed to be breastfed. By incorporating incremental sections of dentine (i.e., the portion of the tooth that incorporates dietary protein), or sampling across various ages within a sample, researchers can identify when nitrogen values are above threshold, indicating breastfeeding, and when the nitrogen values start to drop to match adult average values, from which they infer when weaning occurred (e.g., Smith *et al.* 2023; Salahuddin & Prowse 2023).

7 Trauma and Child Abuse

The study of trauma in past skeletal populations provides information on occupation, personal relationships, mortuary behaviour, accidents, subsistence, and medical intervention. Violence and trauma have long been of interest to bioarchaeologists, yet past analyses focus largely on adults (Martin and Harrod 2015). However, as children were involved in many aspects of life within a community and performed many subsistence and occupational activities, evidence for trauma in their remains can help us explore questions such as the age of apprenticeships, child abuse, parental care, and conditions within their physical environment (e.g., Van de Vijver 2019).

The identification of trauma in non-adult skeletons is rare compared to the rates recorded in adult samples, but trauma still occurs within non-adult populations (Lewis 2007). In our modern world, trauma is among the leading causes of death in individuals under the age of five (along with infectious diseases, preterm birth complications, birth asphyxia, and congenital anomalies), and trauma is the leading cause of death in individuals aged five to fourteen (WHO 2022a, 2022b). In the modern world, trauma in young people often includes car accidents, accidental falls, intentional abuse, and sports injuries. In the past, child's play, apprenticeships, warfare, and intentional abuse would all expose children to trauma (Halcrow and Tayles 2011; Fibiger 2014).

When examining trauma in non-adults, there are a few additional challenges or things we need to keep in mind. The first is the plastic nature of non-adult skeletal remains or pediatric bones (Van de Vijver 2019). That is, non-adult bones contain a greater organic component than adult bones, leaving them more resilient to fracture. As a result, injury to a child (e.g., a fall or car accident) is much more likely to cause fatal soft-tissue injuries than osteological fractures (Martin and Harrod 2015). When looking for evidence of trauma in non-adults, we need to consider that greenstick fractures, buckle fractures, or plastic deformation might be more visible than other forms of fractures. It is also possible that, rather than clean fractures, trauma in non-adults will appear as periosteal bone formation or new bone growth, where agitation of the periosteal surface has occurred. However, as a word of caution, new bone growth can occur for many reasons (e.g., growth, disease), and the presence of periostitis should not immediately be equated to evidence of trauma.

Secondly, the plastic nature of immature bone and rapid repair can mask the subtle bone changes, meaning we may not be able to observe them bioarchaeologically (Van de Vijver 2019). For example, in a twenty-year-old, a femoral fracture may take up to twenty weeks to completely heal. However, if a femoral fracture occurs around the time of birth, healing can take place within three weeks. Some other signs of trauma in non-adults may be visible but create other perceived deformities. For example, a fracture to the end of a diaphysis may result in premature fusing of the epiphysis. Ultimately, this means the long bone will cease linear growth and may appear shorter than the bilateral limb.

Together, this means that fractures may occur less frequently, may appear as other bone alterations (e.g., periosteal new bone formation), or may result in other bony changes (e.g., premature epiphyseal fusion), which should each be considered when examining rates of trauma in non-adults. In regard to trauma, it is important to assess the type of trauma (e.g., blunt force, sharp force), and timing (e.g., before death, after death), as well as the location of the trauma (e.g., proximal third of the femoral shaft), depending on your research questions. Factors associated with the timing of trauma are summarized in the following subsection.

Timing of Trauma

The timing of trauma is often differentiated in relation to the death event, including antemortem (before death), perimortem (around the time of death), and post-mortem (after death) (Christensen *et al.* 2014) (Table 1). These are broad categories that include significant variation. For example, antemortem could include the month before death or twenty years before death. Perimortem could include aspects that contributed to the cause of death, as well as other injuries that occurred shortly before or shortly after death but are unrelated to the death event. Lastly, post-mortem could occur after death while community members are still living, or could include damage inflicted during excavation (e.g., trowel trauma). In the latter example, the damage may not be considered "trauma" but needs to be differentiated from antemortem and perimortem trauma, to help understand trauma and injury, as well as post-mortem environments.

To differentiate between the three timings, key features should be observed. Antemortem trauma should include some evidence of healing whether in the form of new bone growth, a bony callus, or complete unification of the fracture margins. As the bone was alive during this traumatic evidence, the colour should be fairly uniform. Perimortem trauma should also exhibit uniform colouration between the fracture and surrounding bone, but without any evidence of healing. Hinge fractures may be present (Christensen *et al.* 2014). Post-mortem trauma often includes colour differences between the fracture site and the surrounding bone, as the two areas have been exposed to the soils around them for different periods of time.

Table 1 The timing of trauma

Timing	Colour of the fracture area	Evidence of healing	Margins
Antemortem	Uniform between fracture area and surrounding bone	Present (new bone growth, callus, unification of fracture margins, etc.)	Smooth (evidence of healing)
Perimortem	Possible hematoma staining, otherwise uniform	Absent	Sharp but likely uniform
Postmortem	Broken surface is often lighter than the rest of the bone	Absent	Irregular edges due to lack of organic component

A Note on Child Abuse

In 2022, almost 400,000 incidents of physical child abuse were reported to the National Children's Alliance in the United States (National Children's Alliance 2023). In the same year, an estimated 1,990 children died from abuse and/or neglect in the United States alone (National Children's Alliance 2024). The almost complete absence of any reported cases of child abuse in the archaeological record has led many anthropologists to suggest that child abuse, in its current form, is a recent phenomenon. However, the documentary evidence from past societies would suggest otherwise, with literary evidence of corporal punishment and child abuse having been experienced or delivered by many individuals in the past. Thus, the lack of bioarchaeological data regarding child abuse may not stem from a lack of child abuse, but rather, due to our inability to recognize evidence of abuse in non-adult skeletal remains. Unique cases exist (see Wheeler *et al.* 2013 for a well-defined and supported example), but not at the rates we might expect.

Evidence of child abuse is often interpreted from subtle and non-specific lesions that are left behind, contributing to issues associated with differential diagnosis, and the inability to confidently attribute the osteological markers of experiences of trauma (Martin and Harrod 2015). Additionally, it would be inappropriate to define malnutrition as child abuse in contexts where malnutrition was rampant throughout a community. Consequently, much of our knowledge regarding lesions commonly associated with child abuse comes from forensic medical literature.

In a systematic review of published reports concerning skeletal traumatic injuries in individuals under the age of eighteen, Kemp *et al.* (2008) found that no fracture in isolation is indicative of physical abuse, but that there are some consistent patterns that are more common in cases associated with child abuse compared to non-abusive traumatic injuries. These include:

- Presence of multiple fractures
- Presence of rib fractures
- Femoral fracture in those not yet walking
- Humeral fracture in children under the age of three
- Mid-shaft fractures
- Skull fractures, particularly on the parietal or linear skull fractures

Additionally, some features may be of particular interest to bioarchaeologists. For example, multiple fractures exhibiting differential stages of healing may suggest a pattern of repetitive traumatic experiences rather than an isolated incident, corresponding with patterns of continued child abuse rather than an isolated fall or accident (Martin and Harrod 2015). Additionally, new bone formation on the diaphysis of the humerus or radius and ulna may be consistent with the stripping of the periosteum from the bone, which can happen when an individual is forcefully grasped, pulled, or shaken (Caffey 1974).

When looking to the past, it is possible that many of the issues that affect the bioarchaeological studies of childhood more broadly also limit our ability to identify and assess evidence of child abuse. These can include, but are not limited to the following:

1. Burial location: Children who died from abuse may have been buried in clandestine burials, rather than within the general cemetery. As a result, the remains may not be recovered during archaeological excavations.
2. Sample sizes: Based on modern data, an osteological collection of 2,000 infants and children may include one individual who suffered abuse during their life. While large cemetery samples exist in the bioarchaeological record, few include datasets of that size.
3. Preservation: Based on medical data, diagnosis of child abuse relies on the preservation of osteological elements, including the ribs and cranial bones. With fragmentary remains or poorly preserved remains (or improper excavation of complete skeletons), researchers may not have an entire skeleton to examine and assess patterns of trauma across the entire skeleton.

4. Osteological paradox: As evident in statistics from the United States in 2022 (National Children's Alliance 2023), most victims of abuse may survive, and their injuries will heal. Ultimately, this means that evidence of child abuse will remain invisible in the bioarchaeological record.

With this in mind, bioarchaeologists looking to explore experiences of child abuse in the past may need to consider burial locations and associated contexts in which child abuse may have been more prevalent. Examples include examining the remains associated with specific social institutions (e.g., workhouses) or those associated with systems of oppression (e.g., subject to slavery).

8 Adolescence

Adolescents sit at the crossroads of childhood and adulthood. While this has important implications for their social age and experiences within their cultural context, within biological anthropology, this age group is exciting for two particular reasons:

1. Due to the predictable nature of growth and development, adolescents can often be more accurately aged than adults, allowing for small-scale changes to be teased apart and analyzed. This means we might be able to look at rites of passage, or the beginning of gendered treatments in the past with a more fine-tuned approach than we might with adults.
2. Sex estimations are more reliable than for infants and young children, as these individuals are starting to progress through puberty, experiencing sex hormones and developing more sexually derived osteological features. As a result, we can also begin to explore sex-specific patterns within this age group, an approach that is often limited when studying pre-pubertal individuals.

While the bioarchaeological study of adolescence has only recently developed (Lewis 2022; Avery and Lewis 2023; Avery *et al.* 2022), researchers are incorporating more ways to investigate this period of life, including the biological and social changes.

Biological Changes

A major component of the period of adolescence is the biological changes associated with puberty. Puberty is initiated at the hormonal level, generating physical changes in almost every aspect of the body (Hagg and Taranger 1982). Rather than discussing puberty as a single event, researchers often subdivide this period of development into five stages: prepubertal, acceleration, peak height velocity

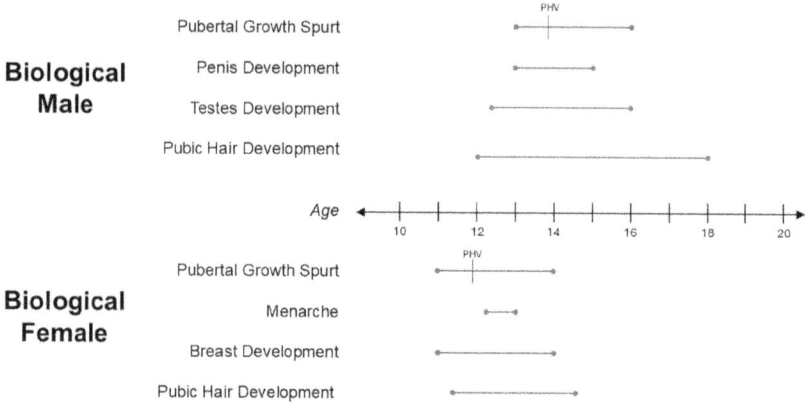

Figure 11 Sequence of pubertal events in boys and girls (adapted from Tanner 1986, 433). PHV – Peak Height Velocity.

(PHV), deceleration, and post-puberty. While the timing and pace through these stages is dependent on many factors (e.g., genetics, nutrition), the general pattern follows a predictable manner (Tanner 1962; Figure 11):

1. Prepuberty encompasses a cascade of hormonal changes, occurring before any morphological changes take place.
2. Acceleration includes the first outward signs of puberty, including breast budding in females and growth of the testes and scrotum in males.
3. Peak Height Velocity (PHV) is the stage in which we see the most amount of outwardly physical changes, including the adolescent growth spurt, with an average height increase of 9.0 cm/year for girls and 10.3 cm/year for boys (Rogol et al., 2002). Menarche (a female's first menstruation) also typically occurs about one year after PHV.
4. Deceleration is when the rate of physical changes begins to slow and corresponds with spermatogenesis and the dropping of the male voice.
5. Post-puberty corresponds to the time when all vertical growth is achieved, and breast and genital development is complete. Some growth in width and breadth (e.g., pelvis), as well as increased musculature may still occur after this point.

While we often associate puberty with changes in soft tissue or hormones, there are several associated osteological changes because skeletal and somatic maturity are influenced by the same biological systems (Dreizen et al. 1967; Ford et al. 2009). Specifically, the pituitary and gonadal secretions responsible for the onset of puberty are also responsible for the ossification of the epiphyseal cartilage and subsequent growth of bones (Demirjian et al. 1985). Saggese et al.

(2002) state that, beyond developing soft tissue, puberty plays a key role for bone development in adolescents.

Pubertal Timing Methods

The use of skeletal maturity to estimate pubertal stage has been most strongly advocated for by orthodontists, as orthodontic treatments (e.g., dental braces, headgear) are most successful when applied during a period of rapid growth, like the pubertal growth spurt (Uysal *et al.* 2006). By looking at key features on x-rays, orthodontists attempt to predict the timing of the pubertal growth spurt, determine the growth velocity during PHV, and estimate the proportion of growth remaining, in order to know when to best apply orthodontic treatments (Santiago *et al.* 2012). Over the years, several skeletal features have been successfully linked with puberty, including hand and wrist maturation, canine mineralization, iliac crest fusion, and cervical vertebrae maturation. Initially applied to x-rays, the methods were subsequently adapted for use on dry bone and summarized by Shapland and Lewis (2013, 2014).

1. Canine

Mandibular canine mineralization is assessed following Demirjian *et al.* (1985), identifying teeth from stages D (crown complete) through H (roots complete) (Figure 12). Using x-rays can help better identify root development in cases where the tooth is in occlusion, otherwise, the root cannot be fully observed and should be recorded as unobservable.

Clinical studies have demonstrated that Demirjian stage F for the mandibular canine correlates with the initiation of puberty, while Demirjian stage G corresponds to immediately prior to PHV (Demirjian *et al.* 1973; Coutinho *et al.* 1993; Chertkow and Fatti 1979). Shapland and Lewis (2013) suggest that stage H coincides with PHV or immediately after.

2. Hamate

The hook of the hamate is assessed following Tanner *et al.* (2001) with the additional stage recommended by Shapland and Lewis (2013), as more subtle changes are observable on dry bone than in clinical x-rays. Stages of hamate development include undeveloped (stage G), appearing (stage H), developing (stage H.5), or complete (stage I) (Figure 13).

According to Chertkow (1980) and Grave and Brown (1976), stage G suggests an individual is prepubertal, while stage H (or H.5) indicates the acceleration stages of pubertal growth spurt, and stage I indicates that PHV has been achieved.

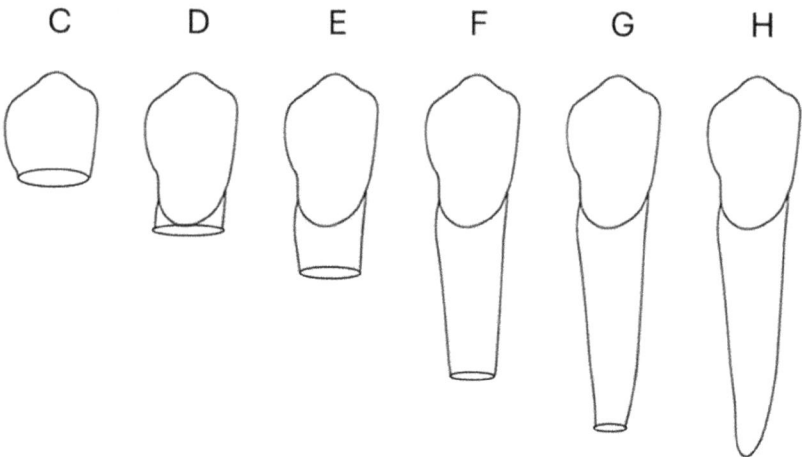

Figure 12 Mineralization of the canine tooth according to Demirjian stages (Demirjian *et al.* 1985). Stage D: Crown complete. Stage E: Crown height is greater than the length of the root. Stage F: Apex ends in a funnel shape; root is greater in length than crown height. Stage G: Apical end is still partly open. Stage H: Apical end of the root canal is completely closed.

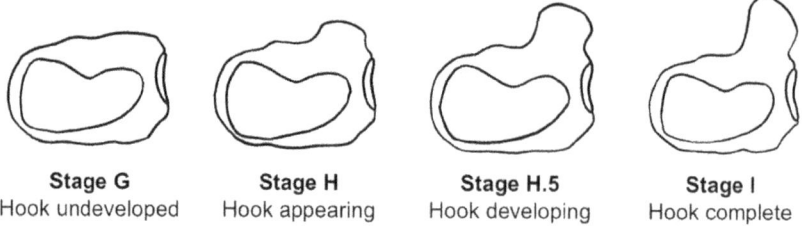

Figure 13 Development of the hook of the hamate.

3. Phalanges

With regards to pubertal status, fusion of the phalanges is assessed as unfused, partially fused, or fused. According to Grave and Brown (1976), the point where the phalangeal epiphyses are equal in width to the metaphysis and begin to cap the metaphysis is correlated with PHV, as is the initial fusion. However, unfused epiphyses are infrequently recovered in archaeological contexts and may not be properly associated to the correct digits. Thus, rather than considering the capping or the width of the unfused epiphyses, fusion of the phalangeal epiphyses is adopted as an indicator that the deceleration phase of puberty had already begun (Hagg and Taranger 1982).

Furthermore, the fusion of the distal phalanx of the second finger has been found to closely correlate with menarche (Buehl and Pyle 1942). However, as this particular digit may be difficult to identify, Shapland and Lewis (2013, 303) suggest that early fusion of the distal phalangeal epiphyses (where a fusion line is still present) indicates that menarche had recently passed, while complete fusion indicates the individual is of a post-menarcheal age.

4. Arm Bones

The distal radius, distal humerus, and proximal ulna are also assessed as unfused, partially fused, or fused. According to Hagg and Taranger (1980, 1982), a fusing distal radius indicates the individual is in the deceleration stage, while complete fusion indicates the individual is post-pubertal. Initial fusion of the proximal ulna and distal humerus corresponds to PHV in both males and females (Roche 1976), suggesting that complete fusion of these elements indicates the deceleration and post-pubertal stages.

5. Iliac Crest

In clinical studies, the amount of ossified but unfused iliac crest is used to differentiate stages of puberty (Risser 1958). However, this is not easily applied in bioarchaeology, as ossified but unfused iliac crests are infrequently recovered due to their fragile nature (Figure 14). Thus, for use in bioarchaeology, a simplified approach is taken, with the iliac crest assessed as unfused and not present, ossified but unfused, fusing, or fused. In this division, an ossified but unfused iliac crest indicates the individual is within the deceleration stage, while complete ossification and fusion indicates the individual is post-pubertal (Biondi *et al.* 1985). However, an unfused and absent iliac crest is not indicative of a particular pubertal stage, as it could have been ossified and simply not recovered archaeologically or may not have begun to ossify at all.

6. Cervical Vertebrae

Cervical vertebrae maturation (CVM) is assessed, following Hassel and Farman (1995), by assessing the general shape and size of the third cervical vertebra (C3). In this method, changes of the cervical body correspond to the entire pubertal growth spurt. However, in clinical and bioarchaeological studies, this method has produced inconsistent results with other pubertal stage indicators (*see* Santiago *et al.* 2012; Arthur *et al.* 2016 for clinical and bioarchaeological studies that discuss this further). One possible explanation for these discrepancies is that CVM divides the period of puberty into six stages rather than five (Ozer *et al.* 2006). Although most clinical researchers recommend combining stages 4 and 5 with the deceleration stage, this inconsistency may contribute to the variable results (Shapland and

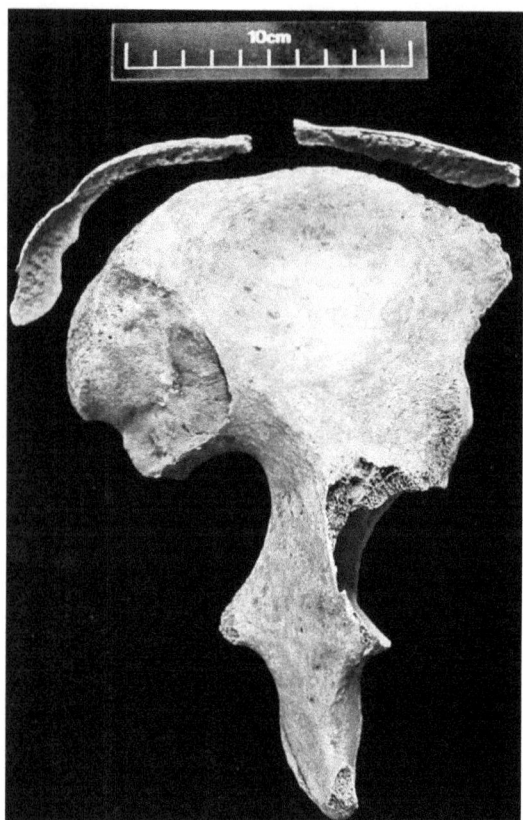

Figure 14 Ossified but unfused iliac crests are rare in the archaeological record, in part due to the fragile nature of the iliac crest that results in significant post-depositional damage. Osteological element from Lisieux-Michelet, France. Photo by author.

Lewis 2014). Within bioarchaeology, it is generally acceptable for the CVM stage to be slightly out-of-line with other pubertal stage indictors, acknowledging the variability and inconsistency associated with this osteological feature. The stages of puberty and observed CVM characteristics are outlined in Table 2.

7. Pubertal Assessment

Once all features are assessed, an individual is placed into a pubertal stage-at-death. Divisions based on six or seven categories are available elsewhere (Falys and Lewis 2020). Table 3, however, provides a division according to five stages. Compared to other approaches, dividing data across five categories allows us to maximize sample sizes in each category and more closely

Table 2 Stages of cervical vertebra maturation

Stage	Inferior border	Body shape
Initiation (1)	Flat	Wedge-shaped
Acceleration (2)	Concavity appears	Nearly rectangular
Transition (3)	Developing	Rectangular
Deceleration (4)	Distinct concavity	Nearly square
Maturation (5)	Accentuated concavity	Square
Completion (6)	Deep concavity	Taller than it is wide

Table 3 Pubertal assessment based on osteological features

	Pre-puberty	Acceleration	PHV	Deceleration	Post-puberty
Canine	Stage D–F	Stage G	Stage H	Stage H	Stage H
Hamate	Stage G	Stage H/H.5	Stage I	Stage I	Stage I
Phalanges	Unfused	Unfused	Unfused or partly fused	Partly fused or fused	Fused
Radius	Unfused	Unfused	Unfused	Partly fused	Fused
Ulna	Unfused	Unfused	Partly fused	Fused	Fused
Humerus	Unfused	Unfused	Partly fused	Fused	Fused
Iliac crest	Unfused	Unfused	Unfused	Ossified and unfused	Partly fused or fused
CVM	Stage 1	Stage 2	Stage 3	Stage 4/5	Stage 6

aligns with medical descriptions of puberty according to the Tanner Stages (Marshall and Tanner 1969, 1970) or Sexual Maturity Ratings. To be assigned a pubertal stage, an individual should have at least three features present and in agreement with one another. As CVM is known to produce slightly inconsistent results, it is not considered problematic if CVM is one stage ahead or behind other features. In these instances, priority is given to other features, provided there were enough features to properly assess the pubertal stage.

In some instances, whether due to small sample sizes, or fragmentary remains, researchers may need to consider exploring samples based on pre-PHV and post-PHV, rather than by five discrete stages. While this approach hides some of the variability observed within puberty, it can help maximize sample sizes to permit more robust statistical analyses.

Social Changes

As the study of adolescence has only recently developed, the methods currently employed to investigate social age changes are limited. No adolescent-specific bioarchaeological approaches have been developed to date, but rather existing methods are being applied to this particular age group, including mobility isotopes (e.g., Lewis and Montgomery 2023), dietary stable isotopes (e.g., Avery *et al.* 2021, 2023b), analysis of mortuary patterns (e.g., Scott *et al.* 2023), and investigation of pathological conditions (e.g., Pererva 2017). As the discipline continues to develop and grow, so too will the approaches used to understand this period of the human life course, offering exciting avenues of future research into the lives of adolescents and young people in the past.

9 Future Directions

Since the "birth" of the bioarchaeological study of infants and childhood over fifty years ago, the discipline has developed to incorporate more methods, questions, and theoretical approaches. Reflecting on publication trends, Mays et al. (2017) noted an increase in bioarchaeological research focused on non-adult skeletal remains between 2006 and 2015, with most publications devoted to paleopathology and bone chemistry (e.g., stable isotopes). Much of this work was driven by methodological advancements, including incorporation of incremental analysis in stable isotope analysis, and identifying pathological lesions associated with non-adults (Mays et al. 2017). Since 2017, continued methodological developments have contributed to the expansion of the field, but so too have the application of theoretical models. By incorporating theories of allostatic load (Temple & Edes 2022), mother–infant nexus (Gowland and Halcrow 2020), Development Origins of Health and Disease (DOHaD) (Gowland 2015), and more, researchers are demonstrating that the study of infants and children has the potential to tell us much more about society in the past.

As we look to the future of the bioarchaeology of infants and children, it is clear that researchers are continuing to push the boundaries of our discipline and find new and innovative ways to study infants and children in the past, including methodological developments (e.g., ancient DNA and proteomics), and the incorporation of further theoretical frameworks (e.g., mother–infant nexus). A few of the newly developing areas, or areas that would benefit from more concentrated attention, are outlined below.

Perinatal Bioarchaeology

As we continue to consider the lives of non-adults, bioarchaeologists are exploring those at the periphery with greater interest. To date, this has included a wave of research regarding adolescents (e.g. see special issue *Bioarchaeology International: Emerging Adolescence*, edited by Creighton Avery, Megan Brickley, and Mary Lewis); however, the youngest members of society remain elusive, existing "on the margins of discussion" (Hodson 2021). Fetal, perinatal, and infants are often viewed as those without agency or identity, as they have not necessarily lived within their communities, societies, or households (Halcrow 2019). However, as Hodson (2021) highlights, these individuals uniquely capture both social and biological data. Biologically, their bodies capture *in utero* conditions, often reflecting maternal health conditions. In a study of perinatal remains from the Spring Street Presbyterian Church burial vaults (New York City; 19th century CE), Ellis (2020) identified perinatal remains, including a mother–infant pair (based on osteological remains and corresponding records). The remains of the mother exhibit evidence of a cariogenic diet and tobacco staining along their teeth; the infant in the same burial was likely exposed to the same harmful substances (Ellis 2020, 197).

Socially, the burial of a perinate may speak to the treatment of the youngest and most vulnerable members of a community (Scott & Betsinger 2021). In a study of a burial associated with the Middle Holocene in Brazil, Solari and colleagues (2020) discuss the remains of perinatal remains that were afforded the same burial treatment as other non-adults and adults within the burial complex, suggesting a level of social identity within its group.

By capturing biological and social conditions, analysis of perinatal remains can provide unparalleled insights into pre- and post-natal experiences within different sociocultural, temporal, and economic environments. Methodological developments in terms of age estimation, growth disruptions, and pathology will contribute to our ability to understand these youngest members, and allow us new avenues of exploration, such as exploring birth experiences, including stillbirths (Booth *et al.* 2016). During the birthing process and breastfeeding, bacteria enter the gastrointestinal tract. However, stillborn infants, who are not exposed to these bacteria through the gastrointestinal tract, do not have evidence of microstructural changes caused by bacterial bioerosion. A study by Ullinger and colleagues (2022) used micro-CT scans to examine evidence of bioerosion and ancient DNA to assess a biological relationship, concluding that a double burial was, in fact, that of fraternal stillborn twins.

Exploring Childhood in Adult Remains

As we continue to develop biochemical and morphological methods, researchers are identifying new ways to explore experiences of childhood that are trapped or captured in adult remains. The most salient example is that of stable isotopes. Considering that teeth develop during childhood and remain relatively static through adulthood, researchers can extract teeth from individuals who died as adults, but observe isotopic values captured during childhood. Such approaches allow researchers to consider the Osteological Paradox (i.e., by exploring dietary consumption patterns of those that died in childhood, versus those who survived the period of childhood), incorporate more reliable sex estimation methods, and expand sample sizes, if necessary. Beyond biochemical approaches, some pathological conditions or manifestations (e.g., vitamin D deficiency and rickets) may be observed in adult remains, allowing us to consider conditions in childhood that affected later adult life. According to Mays et al. (2017), integrated studies of non-adult and adult skeletal remains will only contribute to a more holistic view of life in the past. Continued approaches to studying the last effects of trauma, occupational changes, and growth disruptions will continue to expand our understanding of childhood for those that survived this often-tumultuous period of life.

10 Recording Forms

Recording forms are available on the following pages, and fillable forms are available online.

Skeleton:_____   Date:_____   Observer:_____

Age Estimation

To ensure the greatest sample size can be included, multiple age methods can be used, acknowledging that not all features are consistently present in bioarchaeological collections. In instances where the various methods produce conflicting results, dental development and eruption should be given priority, followed by epiphyseal fusion, and lastly, linear growth (White & Folkens 2005).

Dental Development and Eruption

Instructions: Examine all present teeth in the deciduous and permanent dentition, recording the state of mineralization and/or eruption (scored 1 to 4; see the following for details). Compare results to the chart to estimate age at death (Gustafson and Koch 1974; chart available in White and Folkens 2012, 367)

Deciduous Dentition					Permanent Dentition			
Maxilla		Mandible			Maxilla		Mandible	
Left	Right	Left	Right	Tooth	Left	Right	Left	Right
				M3				
				M2				
				M1				
				m2/P2				
				m1/P1				
				c/C				
				i2/I2				
				i1/I1				

NA: cannot be assessed. 1: crown mineralization begins. 2: crown complete. 3: eruption. 4: root. complete.

Dental Development Age Estimation	Notes[1]

[1] Consider conditions that may influence ability to assess age based on dental development and eruption. For example, are all teeth observable? Is there any antemortem tooth loss? Is the alveolus missing/damaged?

Epiphyseal Fusion

Instructions: Evaluate all epiphyses and metaphyses, determining whether the epiphysis is unfused (visible growth plate, epiphysis unattached), fusing (epiphyseal line clearly visible, epiphysis attached to metaphysis), or fully fused (epiphysis attached to metaphysis, no growth line visible). Compare results to data provided by Cardoso (2008a, 2008b), or some other relevant population standard, to estimate age at death.

	Clavicle	Humerus	Radius	Ulna	Femur	Tibia	Fibula
Sternal end							
Proximal Epiphysis							
Medial Epicondyle							
Greater Trochanter							
Lesser Trochanter							
Distal Epiphysis							

UF: unfused. PF: partly fused. F: fused.

Epiphyseal Fusion Age Estimation	Notes[2]

[2] Consider conditions that may influence your ability to assess age based on epiphyseal fusion. For example, is there some evidence that the epiphysis was fused but damaged and broken off? How might this influence age estimation?

Long Bone Length

Instructions: Measure, in millimetres (mm) all complete and unfused long bones using an osteometric board. Compare measurements to data provided in the Maresh (1970) Range Tables (updated by Spake & Cardoso 2021) or some other relevant population standard to estimate age at death.

	Femur	Tibia	Fibula	Humerus	Radius	Ulna
Left (mm)						
Right (mm)						
Age Range						

Length recorded in mm.

Long Bone Length Age Estimation	Notes[3]

[3] Consider conditions that may influence your ability to assess age based on long bone length. For example, is there a fracture within the long bone that has altered growth and development? Are there large discrepancies between other age estimations that suggest caution should be used with utilizing this age estimation method?

Age Estimation Summary

Instructions: Compile all results and establish final age-at-death estimate.

Dental Development and Eruption Age Estimation	Long Bone Length Age Estimation	Epiphyseal Fusion Age Estimation

Notes

Skeleton:_____   Date:_____   Observer:_____

Biological Sex Estimation

Pelvic and Cranial Dimorphism

Assess the cranium and pelvis for sexually dimorphic features, as outlined in Buikstra and Ubelaker (1994, 15–21). Note: this method should only be applied for older non-adults, where puberty has likely been reached (see Sanchez and Hoppa [2023] for discussion).

Pelvis			Cranium		
Feature	Left	Right	Feature	Left	Right
Vental Arc			Nuchal Crest		
Subpubic Concavity			Mastoid Process		
Ischiopubic Ramus Ridge			Supraorbital Margin		
Greater Sciatic Notch			Glabella		
Preauricular Sulcus			Mental Eminence		

Following Phenice (1969) and Acsadi and Nemeskeri (1970), as summarized by Buikstra and Ubelaker (1994). See Klales *et al.* (2012) for updated descriptions of features of the pelvis. 1 – female, 2 – probable female, 3 – ambiguous, 4 – probable male, 5 – male.

Pelvic Sex Estimation	Notes[4]
Cranial Sex Estimation	

[4] Consider the completeness of the pelvis and cranium and certainty of assessment. Also consider the age of the individual, and if pelvis and cranial dimorphism are appropriate.

Dental Metrics (Cardoso, 2008c)

Instructions: Using sliding calipers, measure permanent canines and premolars mesio-distally (MD) and frontal-lingually (FL). Measurements should be taken in millimetres (mm) and taken to the nearest 0.01 mm. When possible, the left side should be preferentially selected for consistency. Inter- or intra-observer error measurements should also be taken. Following analysis of the entire sample, sample means are to be calculated, and sectioning points established, as described in Cardoso (2008c).

Tooth	Mandibular			Maxillary		
	Side	MD	FL	Side	MD	FL
Canine						
Premolar 1						
Premolar 2						

MD – mesio-distal, FL – frontal-lingual. Measurements taken in mm.

Dental Metrics Sex Estimations	Notes[5]

[5] Indicate if any teeth were not considered due to factors that may affect measurements (e.g., presence of carious lesions, wear patterns, etc.).

Biological Sex Estimation Summary

Instructions: Compile all results and establish final biological sex estimate.

Pelvic Dimorphism	Cranial Dimorphism	Dental Metrics
Notes[6]		

[6] Note if any teeth were sampled for peptide analysis or aDNA analysis, and details about the tooth.

Skeleton:_____   Date:_____   Observer:_____

Dental Health

Examine dentition (teeth and alveolus, if available), and record the dental presence and presence of carious lesions. You can use standard designations according to Buikstra and Ubelaker (1994, 48–55) or develop your own simplified coding system that captures all required information. For example:

Presence/Absence: P – present, AP – absent, post-mortem loss (tooth absent, alveolus present and open), AA – absent, antemortem loss (tooth absent, alveolus present but complete or partial crypt closure indicates antemortem tooth loss) U – unobservable (tooth and alveolus not present).

Carious lesions according to surface affected: I – interproximal, O – occlusal, R – below the cemento-enamel junction, B – buccal/labial, L – lingual, G – gross (when more than one surface is affected).

Maxillary Dentition

	Left									Right							
	M3	M2	M1	P2	P1	C	I2	I1	I1	I2	C	P1	P2	M1	M2	M3
Presence/Absence																	
Permanent																	
Deciduous																	
Carious Lesions																	
Caries 1																	
Caries 2																	

M = molar, P = premolar, C = canine, I = incisor.

Mandibular Dentition

Mandible	Left									Right							
	M3	M2	M1	P2	P1	C	I2	I1	I1	I2	C	P1	P2	M1	M2	M3
Presence/Absence																
Permanent																
Deciduous																
Carious Lesions																
Caries 1																
Caries 2																

M = molar, P = premolar, C = canine, I = incisor.

Notes

Skeleton:_____   Date:_____   Observer:_____

Adolescence

Pubertal Status

Assess osteological features according to methods summarized by Shapland and Lewis (2013, 2014). See text for illustrations and further details.

Osteological Feature	Left	Right
A. Mandibular Canine Root		
B. Hamate		
C. Phalanges		
D. Distal Radial Fusion		
E. Distal Humeral Fusion		
F. Proximal Ulnar Fusion		
G. Iliac Crest		
H. Cervical Vertebrae		
I. Pubertal Stage		

A. Canine root according to Demirjian (1973) Stages: Stage D: Crown complete. Stage E: Crown height is greater than the length of the root. Stage F: Apex ends in a funnel shape; root is greater in length than the crown height. Stage G: Apical end is still partly open. Stage H: Apical end of the root canal is completely closed

B. Hamate: G – hook undeveloped, H – hook appearing, H.5 – hook developing, I – hook complete.

C. Phalanges: UF – unfused, PF – partly fused, F – fused

D. Distal Radius: UF – unfused, PF – partly fused, F – fused

E. Distal Humerus: UF – unfused, PF – partly fused, F – fused

F. Proximal Ulna: UF – unfused, PF – partly fused, F – fused

G. Ilia Crest: UF – unfused, OS – ossified and unfused, PF – partly fused, F – fused

H. Cervical Vertebra – Stages 1 to 6.

Number of features in agreement[1]	Notes[2]
Final Pubertal Stage	

[1] Three or more features present and in agreement with one another are required to make a final pubertal stage designation.

[2] Discuss if CVM is out of alignment, or other observations that may have affected these features (e.g., fractures, disease processes, preservation, canine in occlusion).

Bibliography

Acheson, R. (1966). Maturation of the Skeleton. In F. Faulkner (Ed.), *Human Development*. Philadelphia: Saunders, pp. 465–502.

Agarwal, S., and B. Glencross. (2011). Building a Social Bioarchaeology. In S. Agarwal and B. Glencross (Eds.), *Social Bioarchaeology*. Oxford: Blackwell, pp. 1–12.

Agarwal, S., and J. K. Wesp (Eds.). (2017). *Exploring Sex and Gender in Bioarchaeology*. London: Blackwell.

Amoroso, A., and S. J. Garcia. (2018). Can Early Life Growth Disruptions Predict Longevity? Testing the Association between Vertebral Neural Canal (VNC) Size and Age-at-Death. *International Journal of Paleopathology* 22 (Sept): 8–17. DOI: https://doi.org/10.1016/j.ijpp.2018.03.007.

Ariès, P. (1962). *Centuries of Childhood: A Social History of Family Life*. New York: Vintage Books.

Arthur, N., R. Gowland, and R. Redfern. (2016). Coming of Age in Roman Britain: Osteological Evidence for Pubertal Timing. *American Journal of Physical Anthropology* 159(4): 698–713. DOI: https://doi.org/10.1002/ajpa.22929.

Audsley, B., and M. Khan. (October 2024). *Atlas software app*. Accessed electronically: www.qmul.ac.uk/dentistry/atlas/software-app/. Last accessed December 12, 2024.

Avery, L. C., M. Brickley, S. Findlay, C. Chapelain de Seréville-Niel, and T. Prowse. (2021). Child and Adolescent Diet in Late Roman Gaul: An Investigation of Incremental Dietary Stable Isotopes in Tooth Dentine. *International Journal of Osteoarchaeology* 31(6): 1226–1236. DOI: https://doi.org/10.1002/oa.3033.

Avery, L. C., T. Prowse, and M. Brickley. (2019). Dental health and dietary difference at Late Roman Winchester. *Bioarchaeology International*. 3(30): 157–173. DOI: https://doi.org/10.5744/bi.2019.1011.

Avery, L. C., T. Prowse, S. Findlay, and M. Brickley. (2022). Bioarchaeological Approaches to the Study of Adolescence. *Childhood in the Past* 15(1): 3–14. DOI: https://doi.org/10.1080/17585716.2022.2055865.

Avery, L. C., M. Brickley, S. Findlay, L. Bondioli, A. Sperduti, and T. Prowse. (2023b). Eating Like Adults: An Investigation of Dietary Change in Childhood and Adolescence at *Portus Romae* (Italy, 1st–4th Centuries CE). *Bioarchaeology International: Emerging Adolescence* 7(2). DOI: https://doi.org/10.5744/bi.2022.0006.

Baker, B., T. Dupras, and M. Tocheris. (2005). *The Osteology of Infants and Children*. College Station: Texas A&M University Press.

Baxter, J. (2008). The Archaeology of Childhood. *Annual Review of Anthropology* 37 (2008): 159–175.

Baxter, J. (2019). How to die a good death: Teaching young children about mortality in nineteenth century America. *Childhood in the Past* 12(1): 35-49. DOI: 10.1080/175716.2019.1587913.

Beauchesne, P., and S. C. Agarwal. (2018). *Children and Childhood in Bioarchaeology*. Gainesville: University Press of Florida.

Biehler-Gomez, L., M. Mattia, M. Mondellini, L. Palazzolo, and C. Cattaneo. (2022). Differential Skeletal Preservation between Sexes: A Diachronic Study in Milan over 2000 Years. *Archaeological and Anthropological Sciences* 14 (2022): 147. DOI: https://doi.org/10.1007/s12520-022-01616-0.

Bogin, B. (1999). *Patterns of Human Growth*. Cambridge: Cambridge University Press.

Booth, T. J., R. C. Redfern, and R. L. Gowland. 2016. Immaculate Conceptions: Micro-CT Analysis of Diagenesis in Romano-British Infant Skeletons. *Journal of Archaeological Science* 74 (October): 124–134.

Brzobohatá, H., F. Velimsky, and J. Frolik. (2023). Early Stress Variation Reflected in Adult Vertebral Neural Canal Size within a Medieval Silver-Mining Population from Kutna Hora (Czech Republic). *Anthropological Science* 123(2): 151–162. DOI: https://doi.org/10.1537/ase.231017.

Buckberry, J. (2005). Where Have All the Children Gone? The Preservation of Infant and Children's Remains in the Archaeological Record. Paper presented at The Archaeology of Infancy and Childhood conference, May 6–8, 2005. Kent: University of Kent.

Buikstra, J., and D. Cook. (1980). Paleopathology: An American Account. *Annual Review of Anthropology* 9: 433–470.

Buikstra, J., and D. Ubelaker. (1994). *Standards for Data Collection from Human Skeletal Remains: Proceedings of a Seminar at the Field Museum of Natural History* (Arkansas Archaeology Research Series 44). Fayetteville, AR: Archaeological Survey.

Buonasera, T., J. Eerkns, A. de Flamingh, L. Engbring, J. Yip, H. Li, R. Haas, D. DiGiuseppe, D. Grant, M. Salemi, C. Nijmeh, M. Arellano, A. Leventhal, B. Phinney, B. F. Byrd, R. S. Malhi, and G. Parker. (2020). A Comparison of Proteomic, Genomic, and Osteological Methods of Archaeological Sex Estimation. *Nature: Scientific Reports* 10:11897. DOI: https://doi.org/10.1038/s41598-020-68550-w.

Caffey J. (1974). The Whiplash Shaken Infant Syndrome: Manual Shaking by the Extremities with Whiplash-Induced Intracranial and Intraocular Bleeding, Linked with Residual Permanent Brain Damage and Metal Retardation. *Pediatrics* 54: 396–403.

Cardoso, H. (2008a). Epiphyseal Union at the Innominate and Lower Limb in a Modern Portuguese Skeletal Sample, and Age Estimation in Adolescent and Young Adult Male and Female Skeletons. *American Journal of Physical Anthropology* 135(2): 161–170. DOI: https://doi.org/10.1002/ajpa.20717.

Cardoso, H. (2008b). Age Estimation of Adolescent and Young Adult Male and Female Skeletons II, Epiphyseal Union at the Upper Limb and Scapular Girdle in a Modern Portuguese Skeletal Sample. *American Journal of Physical Anthropology* 137(1): 97–105. DOI: https://doi.org/10.1002/ajpa.20850.

Cardoso, H. (2008c). Sample Specific (Universal) Metric Approaches for Determining the Sex of Immature Human Skeletal Remains Using Permanent Tooth Dimensions. *Journal of Archaeological Science* 35(1): 158–168. DOI: https://doi.org/10.1016/j.jas2007.02.013.

Chertkow, S. (1980). Tooth Mineralization as an Indicator of the Pubertal Growth Spurt. *American Journal of Orthodontics* 77(1): 79–91. DOI: https://doi.org/10.1016/0002-9416(80)90226-2.

Chertkow, S., and P. Fatti. (1979). The Relationship Between Tooth Mineralization and Early Radiographic Evidence of the Ulnar Sesamoid. *The Angle Orthodontist* 49(4): 282–288.

Cheverko, C. (2020). "Life Course Approaches and Life History Theory: Synergistic Perspectives for Bioarchaeology". In Cheverko *et al.* (Eds.), *Theoretical Approaches in Bioarchaeology* (pp. 59–75).

Cheverko, C. M., J. R. Prince-Buitenhuys, and M. Hubbe. (2021). *Theoretical Approaches in Bioarchaeology*. London: Routledge Taylor & Francis Group.

Christensen, A. M., N. V. Passalacqua, and E. J. Bartelink. (2014). *Forensic Anthropology: Current Methods and Practice*. New York: Academic Press.

Claassen, C. (Ed.). (1992). *Exploring Gender through Archaeology: Selected Papers from the 1991 Boone Conference*. Madison, WI: Prehistory Press.

Clark, G., N. Hall, G. Amelagos, G. B, M. Panjabi, and F. Wetzel. (1986). Poor Growth prior to Early Childhood: Decreased Health and Lifespan in the Adult. *American Journal of Physical Anthropology* 70(2): 145–160.

Cootes, K., M. Thomas, D. Jordan, J. Axworthy, and R. Carlin. (2020). Blood Is Thicker Than Baptismal Water: A Late Medieval Perinatal Burial in a Small Household Chest. *International Journal of Osteoarchaeology* 31(3): 358–365. DOI: https://doi.org/10.1002/oa.2955.

Coutinho, S., P. Buschang, and F. Miranda. (1993). Relationships between Mandibular Canine Calcification Stages and Skeletal Maturity. *American Journal of Orthodontics and Dentofacial Orthopedics* 104(3): 262–298. DOI: https://doi.org/10.1016/S0889-5406(05)81728-7.

Cunningham, C., L. Scheuer, S. Black, H. Liversidge, and A. Christie. (2016). *Developmental Juvenile Osteology*. Amsterdam: Elsevier.

Demirjian, A., H. Goldstein, and J. Tanner. (1973). A New System of Dental Age Assessment. *Human Biology* 45(2): 211–227.

Demirjian, A., P. Buschang, R. Tanguay, and P. Kingnorth. (1985). Interrelationships among Measures of Somatic, Skeletal, Dental and Sexual Maturity. *American Journal of Orthodontics* 88(5): 433–438. DOI: https://doi.org/10.1016.0002-9416(85)90070-3.

Dhavale, N., S. Halcrow, H. Buckley, N. Tayles, K. Domett, and A. Gray. (2017). Linear and Appositional Growth in Infants and Children from the Prehistoric Settlement of Ban Non Wat, Northeast Thailand: Evaluating Biological Responses to Agricultural Intensification in Southeast Asia. *Journal of Archaeological Science: Reports* 11(2017): 435–446. DOI: https://doi.org/10.1016/j.jasrep.2016.12.019.

Dreizen, S., C. Spirakis, and R. Stone. (1967). A Comparison of Skeletal Growth and Maturation in Undernourished and Well-Nourished Girls before and after Menarche. *The Journal of Pediatrics* 70(2): 256–263.

Ellis, M. (2020). Still life: A Bioarchaeological Portrait of Perinatal Remains Buried at the Spring Street Presbyterian Church. *Historic Archaeology* 54-(2020): 184–201. DOI: https://doi.org/10.1007/s41636-019-00216-5.

Eyben, E. (1972). Antiquity's View of Puberty. *Latomus* 31(3): 677–697.

Falys, C., and M. Lewis (2020). Puberty in the Past. *The Archaeologist* 109: 10–11.

Falys, C., H. Schutkowski, and D. Weston. (2005). The Distal Humerus: A Blind Test of Rogers' Sexing Technique Using a Documented Skeletal Collection. *Journal of Forensic Science* 50(6): 1289–1294. DOI: https://doi.org/10.1520/JFS2005171.

Fausto-Sterling, A., C. Garcia Coll, and M. Lamarre. (2012). Sexing the Baby: Part 1 – What Do We Really Know about Sex Differentiation in the First Three Years of Life? *Social Science Medicine* 74(11): 1684–1692.

Fibiger, L. (2014). Misplaced Childhood? Interpersonal Violence and Children in Neolithic Europe. In M. Smith and C. Knusel (Eds.), *The Routledge Handbook of the Bioarchaeology of Human Conflict*. Abingdon: Routledge, pp. 127–145.

Ford, K., J. Khoury, and F. Biro. (2009). Early Markers of Pubertal Onset: Height and Foot Size. *Journal of Adolescent Health* 44(5): 500–501.

Gamble, J., and G. Bentley. (2022). Developmental Origins of Health and Disease (DOHaD): Perspectives from Bioarchaeology. In K. A. Plomp et al. (Eds.), *Palaeopathology and Evolutionary Medicine*. Oxford: Oxford University Press, pp. 17–41.

Garland, C. J. (2020). Implications of Accumulative Stress Burdens during Critical Periods of Early Postnatal Life for Mortality Risk among Guale Interred in a Colonial Era Cemetery in Spanish Florida (ca. AD 1605–1680. *American Journal of Biological Anthropology* 172(4): 621–637. DOI: https://doi.org/10.1002/ajpa.24020.

Geller, P. (2008). Conceiving Sex: Fomenting a Feminist Bioarchaeology. *Journal of Social Archaeology*. 8(1): 113–138. DOI: https://doi.org/10.1177/1469605307086080.

Geller, P. (2021). *Theorizing Bioarchaeology*. In D. L. Martin (Series Ed.). Bioarchaeology and Social Theory. London: Springer.

Gero, J. M., and M. W. Conkey (Eds.) (1991). *Engendering Archaeology: Women and Prehistory*. Cambridge, MA: Blackwell.

Gilchrist, R. (2022). Voices from the Cemetery: The Social Archaeology of Late-Medieval Burial. *Medieval Archaeology* 66(1): 120–150. DOI: https://doi.org/10.1080/00766097.2022.2003610.

Goodman, A., and G. Armelagos. (1989). Infant and Childhood Morbidity and Mortality Risks in Archaeological Populations. *World Archaeology* 21 (2): 225–243.

Goodman, A., and T. Leatherman (1998). *Building a New Biocultural Synthesis: Political-Economic Perspectives of Human Biology*. Ann Arbor: The University of Michigan Press.

Gowland, R. (2006). Ageing the past: Examining age identity from funerary evidence. In R. Gowland and C. Knusel (Eds.), *The social archaeology of funerary remains*. Barnsley, UK: Oxbow Books, pp. 143–154.

Gowland, R. (2015). Entangled Lives: Implications for the Developmental Origins of Health and Disease Hypothesis for Bioarchaeology and the Life Course. *American Journal of Physical Anthropology* 158(4): 530–540.

Gowland, R. (2017). Embodied Identities in Roman Britain: A Bioarchaeological Approach. *Britannia*. DOI: https://doi.org/10.1017/S0068113X17000125.

Gowland, R., and J. Caldwell. (2022). The Developmental Origins of Health and Disease. *The Routledge Handbook of Paleopathology*. London: Routledge. DOI: https://doi.org/10.4324/9781003130994.

Gowland, R., and S. Halcrow. (2020). *The Mother–Infant Nexus in Anthropology: Small Beginnings, Significant Outcomes*. Cham: Springer. DOI: https://doi.org/10.1007/978-3-030-27393-4.

Gowland, R., N. A. Stewart, K. D. Crowder, C. Hodson, H. Shaw, K. J. Gron, and J. Montgomery. (2021). Sex Estimation of Teeth at Different Developmental Stages Using Dimorphic Enamel Peptide Analysis. *American Journal of Biological Anthropology* 174(4): 859–869. DOI: https://doi.org/10.1002/akpa.24231.

Grave, K., and T. Brown. (1976). Skeletal Ossification and the Adolescent Growth Spurt. *American Journal of Orthodontics* 69(6): 611–619. DOI: https://doi.org/10.1016/0002-9416(76)90143-3.

Greulich W., and S. Pyle. (1950). *Radiographic atlas of skeletal development of the hand and wrist*. Standford University Press.

Gustafson, G., and G. Koch. (1974). Age Estimation up to 16 Years of Age based on Dental Development. *Odontologisk Revy* 25(3): 297–306.

Gutierrez, E., I. Ribot, and J.-F. Helie. (2021). Weaning among Colonists from Montreal and Environs: What Can Nitrogen Isotope Analysis on Dentine Tell Us? *Bioarchaeology International* 5(3–4): 124–142. DOI: https://doi.org/10.5744/bi.2020.0022.

Hagg, U., and J. Taranger. (1980). Menarcheal and Voice Change as Indicators of the Pubertal Growth Spurt. *Acta Odontologica Scandinavica* 38(3): 179–186. DOI: https://doi.org/10.3109/00016358009004718.

Hagg, U., and J. Taranger. (1982). Maturation Indicators and the Pubertal Growth Spurt. *American Journal of Orthodontics* 82(4): 299–309. DOI: https://doi.org/10.1016/0002-9416(82)90464-X.

Halcrow, S. (2019). Infants in the Bioarchaeological Past: Who Cares? In R. Gowland and S. Halcrow (Eds.) The Mother–Infant Nexus in Anthropology: Small Beginnings, Significant Outcomes. Cham: Springer, pp. 19–38.

Halcrow, S., and N. Tayles. (2008). The Bioarchaeological Investigation of Childhood and Social Age: Problems and Prospects. *Journal of Archaeological Method and Theory* 15(2008): 190–215. DOI: https://doi.org/10.1007/s10816-008-9052-x.

Halcrow, S., and N. Tayles. (2011). The Bioarchaeological Investigation of Children and Childhood. In S. C. Agarwal and B. A. Glencross (Eds.), *Social Bioarchaeology*, pp. 333–360. Oxford: Wiley-Blackwell.

Hammond, G., and N. Hammond. (1981). Child's Play: A Distorting Factor in Archaeological Distribution. *American Antiquity* 46(1981): 634–636.

Hassel, B., and A. Farman. (1995). Skeletal Maturation Evaluation Using Cervical Vertebrae. *American Journal of Orthodontics and Dentofacial Orthopedics* 107(1): 58–66. DOI: https://doi.org/10.1016/S0889-5406(95)70157-5.

Hillson, S. (1996). *Dental Anthropology*. Cambridge: Cambridge University Press.

Hillson, S. (2001). Recording Dental Caries in Archaeological Human Remains. *International Journal of Osteoarchaeology* 11(4): 249–289. DOI: https://doi.org/10.1002/oa.538.

Hillson, S. (2008). The Current State of Dental Decay. In *Technique and Application in Dental Anthropology*, edited by Joel D. Irish and Greg C. Nelson. Cambridge: Cambridge University Press, pp. 111–135.

Hillson, S. (2014). *Tooth Development in Human Evolution and Bioarchaeology*. Cambridge: Cambridge University Press.

Hodges, P. C. (1933). An epiphyseal chart. *American Journal of Roentgenology* 30: 809–810.

Hodson, C. (2021). New Prospects for Investigation Early Life-Course Experiences and Health in Archaeological Fetal, Perinatal and Infant Individuals. *Childhood in the Past* 14(1): 3–12. DOI: https://doi.org/10.1080/17585716.2021.19058884.

Holder, S., Z. Miliauskiene, R. Jankauskas, and T. Dupras. (2021). An Interpretive Approach to Studying Plasticity in Growth Disruption and Outcomes: A Bioarchaeological Case Study of Napoleonic Soldiers. *American Journal of Human Biology* 33(2): e23457. DOI: https://doi.org/10.1002.ajhb.23457.

Hollimon, S. (2011). Sex and Gender in Bioarchaeological Research. In S. C. Agarwal and B. A. Glencross (Eds.), *Social Bioarchaeology*. Oxford: Blackwell, pp. 149–182.

Hollimon, S. (2017). Bioarchaeological Approaches to Nonbinary Genders: Case Studies from Native North America. In S. C. Agarwal & J. K. Wesp (Eds.), *Exploring Sex and Gender in Bioarchaeology*. Oxford: Blackwell, pp. 51–69

Hooton, E. (1930). *Indians of Pecos Pueblo: A Study of their Skeletal Remains*. New Haven, CT: Yale University Press.

Inglis, Raelene, and Sian Halcrow. (2018). The bioarchaeology of childhood: Theoretical development in the field. In Patrick Beauchesne and Sabrina Agarwal (Eds.), *Children and Childhood in Bioarchaeology*. Gainesville, FL: University Press of Florida, pp. 33–60.

Jimenez del Val, Nasheli. (2009). Seeing cannibals: European colonial discourses on the Latin American other. PhD thesis, Cardiff University.

Johnston, F. (1962). Growth of Long Bones in Infants and Young Children at Indian Knoll. *American Journal of Physical Anthropology* 20(3): 249–254.

Joyce, R. (2005). Archaeology of the Body. *Annual Review of Anthropology* 34(1): 139–158.

Kamp, K. (2001). Where Have All the Children Gone? The Archaeology of Childhood. *Journal of Archaeological Method and Theory* 8(1): 1–34. DOI: https://doi.org/10.1023.a:1009562531188.

Katzenberg, M., and A. Waters-Rist. (2019). Stable Isotope Analysis: A Tool for Studying Past Diet, Demography and Life History. In M. A. Katzenberg and A. L. Grauer (Eds.), *Biological Anthropology of the Human Skeleton, Third Edition*. Oxford: Wiley Blackwell, pp. 469–504.

Kemp, A., F. Dunstan, S. Harrison, S. Morris, M. Mann, K. Rolfe, S. Datta, D. Thomas, J. Sibert, and S. Maguire. (2008). Patterns of Skeletal Fractures in Child Abuse: Systematic Review. *BMJ* 337: a1518. DOI: https://doi.org/10.1136/bmj.a1518.

Kenyhercz, Michael W., A. R. Klales, J. E. Stull, K. A. McCormick, and S. J. Cole. (2017). Worldwide Population Variation in Pelvic Sexual Dimorphism: A Validation and Recalibration of the Klales et al. Method. *Forensic Science International* 227: 259.31–259.e8. DOI: https://doi.org/10.1016/j.forsciint.2017.05.001.

Klales, A. R., S. D. Ousley, and J. M. Vollner. (2012). A Revised Method of Sexing the Human Innominate using Phenice's Nonmetric Traits and Statistical Methods. *American Journal of Physical Anthropology* 149(1): 104–114. DOI: https://doi.org/10.1002/ajpa.22102.

Lally, M. (2008). Bodies, Bones, Objects and Stones: Investigating Infancy, Infant Death, Deposition and Human Identity in Iron Age Southern England. Unpublished PhD thesis, University of Southampton.

Lewis, M. (2007). *The Bioarchaeology of Children: Perspectives from Biological and Forensic Anthropology*. Cambridge: Cambridge University Press.

Lewis, M. (2019). Children in Bioarchaeology: Methods and Interpretations. In M. A. Katzenberg and A. L. (Eds.), *Biological Anthropology of the Human Skeleton*. Hoboken: Wiley & Sons, pp. 119–144.

Lewis, M. (2022). Exploring Adolescence as a Key Life History Stage in Bioarchaeology. *American Journal of Biological Anthropology* 179(4): 519–534. DOI: https://doi.org/10.1002/ajpa.24615.

Lewis, M., and J. Montgomery. (2023). Youth Mobility, Migration, and Health before and after the Black Death. *Bioarchaeology International: Emerging Adolescence* DOI: https://doi.org/5744/bi.2022.0015.

Lillehammer, G. (1989). A Child Is Born: The Child's World in an Archaeological Perspective. *Norwegian Archaeological Review* 22:2, 89–105. DOI: https://doi.org/10.1080/00293652.1989.9965496.

Liston, M., and J. Papadopoulos. (2004). The "Rich Athenian Lady" Was Pregnant: The Anthropology of a Geometric Tomb Reconsidered. *Hesperia* 73(1): 7–38.

Liston, M., and S. Rotroff. (2013). Babies in the Well: Archaeological Evidence for Newborn Disposal in Hellenistic Greece. J. E. Grubbs and T. Parkin

(Eds.), *The Oxford Handbook of Childhood and Education in the Classical World*. DOI: https://doi.org/10.1093/oxfordhb/9780199781546.013.003.

Liversidge, H., J. Buckberry, and N. Marquez-Grant. (2015). Age Estimation. *Annals of Human Biology* 42(4): 299–301. DOI: https://doi.org/10.3109/03014460.2015.1089627.

Lugli, F., C. Figus, S. Silvestrini, V. Costa, E. Bortolini, S. Conti, B. Peripoli, A. Nava, A. Sperduti, L. Lamanna, L. Bondioli, and S. Benazzi. (2020). Sex-Related Morbidity and Mortality in Non-adult Individuals from the Early Medieval site of Valdaro (Italy): The Contribution of Dental Enamel Peptide Analysis. *Journal of Archaeological Science: Reports* 34(2020): 102625. DOI: https://doi.org/10.1016/j.jasrep.2020.102625.

Lukacs, J. (2008). Fertility and Agricultura Accentuate Sex Differences in Dental Caries Rates. *Current Anthropology* 49(5): 901–914. DOI: https://doi.org/10.1086/592111.

Lukacs, J. (2009). Markers of Physiological Stress in Juvenile Bonobos (*Pan paniscus*): Are Enamel Hypoplasia, Skeletal Development, and Tooth Size Interrelated? *American Journal of Physical Anthropology* 139(3): 339–352. DOI: https://doi.org/10.1002/ajpa.20990.

Maass, C. (2023). Childhood in Captivity: Bioarchaeological Evidence from a Late Colonial Sugar Plantation in Central Peru. *Latin American Antiquity* 34(1): 194–211. DOI: https://doi.org/10.1017/laq.2022.35.

Mahfouz, E. M., E. S. Mohammed, S. F. Alkilany, and T. A. A. Rahman. (2021). The Relationship between Dietary Intake and Stunting among Pre-school Children in Upper Egypt. *Public Health Nutrition* 25(8): 2179–2187. DOI: https://doi.org/10.1017/S136898002100389X.

Maresh, M. (1943). Growth of Major Long Bones in Healthy Children. *American Journal of Diseases of Children* 66(3): 227–257.

Maresh, M. (1955). Linear Growth of Long Bones of Extremities from Infancy through Adolescence. *American Journal of Diseases of Children* 89(6): 725–742.

Maresh, M. (1970). Measurements from Roentgenograms, Heart Size, Long Bone Lengths, Bone, Muscles and Fat Widths, Skeletal Maturation. In R. W. McCammon (Ed.), *Human Growth and Development* Springfield, IL: C. C. Thomas, pp. 155–200.

Marini, N., and G. Flensborg. (2023). Systemic Stress in Hunter-Gatherers from the Central Pampas Dunefields (Argentina): Evaluating Linear Enamel Hypoplasia during the Holocene. *Archaeological and Anthropological Sciences* 15(6): 83. DOI: https://doi.org/10.1007/s12520-023-01781-w.

Marshall, W., and J. Tanner. (1969). Variations in Pattern of Pubertal Changes in Girls. *Archives of Disease in Childhood* 44(235): 291–303. DOI: https://doi.org/10.1136/adc.44.235.291.

Marshall, W., and J. Tanner. (1970). Variations in the Pattern of Pubertal Changes in Boys. *Archives of Disease in Childhood* 45(239): 13–23. DOI: https://doi.org/10.1136/adc.45.239.13.

Martin, D., and R. Harrod. (2015). Bioarchaeological Contributions to the Study of Violence. *Yearbook of Physical Anthropology* 156 (S59): 116–145. DOI: https://doi.org/10.1002/ajpa.22662.

Mays, S. (2001). Sex Identification in Some Putative Infanticide Victims from Roman Britain Using Ancient DNA. *Journal of Archaeological Science* 28(5): 555–559. DOI: https://doi.org/10.1006/jasc.2001.0616.

Mays, S. (2018). The Study of Growth in Skeletal Populations. In S. E. Crawford, D. M. Haldey, and G. B. Shepherd (Eds.), *The Oxford Handbook of the Archaeology of Childhood*. Oxford: Oxford University Press, pp. 71–89.

McFadden, C., B. Muir, and M. Oxenham. (2022). Determinants of Infant Mortality and Representation in Bioarchaeological Samples: A Review. *American Journal of Physical Anthropology* 177(2): 196–206. DOI: https://doi.org/10.1002/ajpa.24406.

Miller, M. J., Y. Dong, K. Pechenkina, W. Fan, and S. E. Halcrow. (2020). Raising Girls and Boys in Early China: Stable Isotope Data Reveal Sex Differences in Weaning and Childhood Diets during the Eastern Zhou Era. *American Journal of Biological Anthropology* 172(4): 567–585. DOI: https://doi.org/10.1002/ajpa.24033.

Miller, M. J., S. C. Agarwal, and C. H. Langebaek. (2018). Dietary Histories: Tracing Food Consumption Practices from Childhood through Adulthood Using Stable Isotope Analysis. In P. Beauchesne and S. Agarwal (Eds.), *Children and Childhood in Bioarchaeology*. Gainesville, FL: University of Florida Press, pp. 262–293.

Moore, W., and M. Corbett. (1971). Distribution of Dental Caries in Ancient British populations: I Anglo-Saxon Period. *Caries Research* 5(2): 151–168. DOI: https://doi.org/10.1159/000259743.

Moore, W., and M. Corbett. (1973). Distribution of Dental Caries in Ancient British Populations: II Iron Age, Romano-British and Medieval Period. *Caries Research* 7(2): 139–153. DOI: https://doi.org/10.1159/000259838.

Moorrees, C., E. Fanning, and E. Hunt. (1963). Age Variation of Formation Stages for Ten Permanent Teeth. *Journal of Dental Research* 42(6): 1490–1502.

Murphy, E. M. (2011). Children's Burial Grounds in Ireland (*Cillini*) and Parental Emotions toward Infant Death. *International Journal of Historic Archaeology* 15(2011): 409–428. DOI: https://doi.org/10.1007/s10761-011-0148-8.

Murphy, E., and M. Le Roy (Eds.). (2017). *Children, Death, and Burial: Archaeological Discourses*. Barnsley, UK: Oxbow Books.

National Children's Alliance. (2023). *National CAC Statistics*. Accessed electronically: www.nationalchildrensalliance.org/wp-content/uploads/2024/03/24_NCA005_Annual_CAC_Stats_F-2.pdf. Last accessed August 30, 2024.

National Children's Alliance. (2024). *National Statistics on Child Abuse*. Accessed electronically: www.nationalchildrensalliance.org/media-room/national-statistics-on-child-abuse/. Last accessed August 30, 2024.

Nava, A. (2024). Understanding the Mother–Infant Nexus from Dental Histology and High-Resolution Compositional Biogeochemistry: Implications for Bioarchaeological Research. *Bulletins et memoires de la societe d'anthropologie de Paris* 36(1): 10–21. DOI: https://doi.org/10.4000/bmsap.13828.

Newman, S. L., and R. L. Gowland. (2015). Brief Communication: The Use of Non-adult Vertebral Dimensions as Indicators of Growth Disruption and Non-specific Health Stress in Skeletal Populations. *American Journal of Physical Anthropology* 158(1): 155–164. DOI: https://doi.org/10.1002/ajpa.22770.

Nikitovic, D. (2017). Embodiment of Puebloan Childhoods: Towards a Bioarchaeology of Childhood. Unpublished doctoral dissertation, Department of Anthropology, Toronto: University of Toronto.

O'Connell, L. (2004). Guidance on recording age at death in adults. In M. Brickley and J. I. McKinley (Eds.), *Guidelines to the Standards for Recording Human Remains*. Southampton, UK: British Association for Biological Anthropology and Osteoarchaeology, pp. 18–20.

Olivier, G., and H. Pineau. (1960). Nouvelle détermination de la taille foetal d'apres les longueurs diaphysaires des os long. *Annales de médecine légale* 68 (51): 141–144.

Ozer, T., J. Jama, and S. Ozer. (2006). A Practical Method for Determining Pubertal Growth Spurt. *American Journal of Orthodontics and Dentofacial Orthopedics* 130(2): 131.e1–131.e6. DOI: https://doi.org/10.1016/j.ajodo.2006.01.019.

Parker, G. J., J. M. Yip, J. W. Eerkens, M. Salemi, B. Durbin-Johnson, C. Kiesow, R. Haas, J. E. Buisktra, H. Klaus, L. A. Regan, D. M. Rocke, and B. S. Phinney. (2019). Sex estimation using sexually dimorphic amelogenin protein fragments in human enamel. *Journal of Archaeological Science* 101(2019): 169–180. DOI: https://doi.org/10.1016/j.jas.2018.08.011.

Pererva, Evgeniy. (2017). Child and Adolescent Paleo-anthropological Materials of Late Sarmatian Time from the Burial Mounds of the Lower Volga Region. *The Lower Volga Archaeological Bulletin* 16(1): 83–108.

Perry, M. (2005). Redefining Childhood through Bioarchaeology: Toward an Archaeological and Biological Understanding of Children in Antiquity. *Archaeological Papers of the American Anthropological Association* 15(1): 89–111.

Phenice, T. (1969). A Newly Developed Visual Method of Sexing the Os Pubis. *American Journal of Physical Anthropology* 30(2): 297–301. DOI: https://doi.org/10.1002/ajpa.1330300214.

Pokines J., and J. De La Paz. (2015). Recovery rates of human fetal skeletal remains using varying mesh sizes. *Journal of Forensic Science* 61: 184–189.

Prowse, T., S. Saunders, H. Schwarcz, P. Garnsey, R. Macchiarelli, and L. Bondioli. (2008). Isotopic and Dental Evidence for Infant and Young Child Feeding Practices in an Imperial Roman Skeletal Sample. *American Journal of Physical Anthropology* 137(3): 294–308.

Reid, D. J., and M. C. Dean. (2006). Variation in Modern Human Enamel Formation Times. *Journal of Human Evolution* 50(3): 329–346. DOI: https://doi.org/10.1016/j.jhevol.2005.09.003.

Richards, M. P., B. T. Fuller, and T. I. Molleson. (2006). Stable Isotope Palaeodietary Study of Humans and Fauna from the Multi-period (Iron Age, Viking and Late Medieval) Site of Newark Bay, Orkney. *Journal of Archaeological Science* 33(1): 122–131. DOI: https://doi.org/10.1016/j.jas.2005.07.003.

Risser, J. (1958). The Iliac Apophysis: An Invaluable Sign in the Management of Scoliosis. *Clinical Orthopaedics* 11(1958): 111–119.

Roch, A. (1976). Growth after Puberty. In E. Fuchs (Ed.). *Youth in a Changing World: Cross-Cultural Perspectives on Adolescence*. New York: Walter de Gruyter, pp. 8–17.

Rogers, T. (1999). A Visual Method of Determining the Sex of Skeletal Remains Using the Distal Humerus. *Journal of Forensic Sciences* 44(1): 57–60.

Rogers, T. (2009). Sex Determination of Adolescent Skeletons Using the Distal Humerus. *American Journal of Physical Anthropology*: 140(1): 143–148. DOI: https://doi.org/10.1002/ajpa.21060.

Rogol, A., K. Roemmich, and P. Clark. (2002). Growth at Puberty. *Journal of Adolescent Health* 31(6): 192–200. DOI: https://doi.org/10.1016/S1054-139X(02)00485-8.

Ruff, C. (2007). Body Size Prediction from Juvenile Skeletal Remains. *American Journal of Physical Anthropology* 133(1): 698–716. DOI: https://doi.org/10.1002/ajpa.20568.

Ruff, C., E. Garofalo, and M. Holmes. (2013). Interpreting Skeletal Growth in the Past from a Functional and Physiological Perspectives. *American Journal of Physical Anthropology* 150(1): 29–37. DOI: https://doi.org/10.1002/ajpa.22120.

Sadler, K. (2017). In M. A. Goldstein (Ed.), *The MassGen Hospital for Children Adolescent Medicine Handbook, Second Edition*. Cham: Springer. DOI 10.1007/978-3-319-45778-9_3, pp. 19–26.

Saggese, G., G. Baroncelli, and S. Bertelloni. (2002). Puberty and Bone Development. *Best Practice and Research Clinical Endocrinology and Metabolism* 16(1): 53–64.

Salahuddin, H., and T. Prowse. (2023). Multi-tissue Analysis of Breastfeeding and Weaning in Iron Age (Seventh–Fourth c. BC) South Italy. *Bioarchaeology International* 7(3): 234–264. DOI: https://doi.org/10.5744/bi.2023.0001.

Sanders, J. O., X. Qiu, X. Lu, D. Duren, R. Liu, D. Dang, M. Mendendez, S. Hansa, D. Weber, and D. Cooperman. (2017). The Uniform Pattern of Growth and Skeletal Maturation during the Human Adolescent Growth Spurt. *Nature: Scientific Reports* 7(1): 16705. DOI: https://doi.org/10.1038/s41598-017-16996-w.

Santiago, R., L. Coasta, R. Vitral, M. Fraga, A. Bolognese, and L. Maia. (2012). Cervical Vertebral Maturation as a Biological Indicator of Skeletal Maturity: A Systematic Review. *Angle Orthodontist* 82(6): 1123–1131. DOI: https://doi.org/10.2319/103111-673.1.

Saunders, Shelley R. (2000). Subadult skeletons and growth-related studies. In: M. Anne Katzenberg and S. Saunders (Eds.), *Biological Anthropology of the Human Skeleton*. Wiley-Liss, pp. 1–20.

Saunders, S. (2008). Subadult skeletons and growth-related studies. In M. Katzenberg and S. Saunders (Eds.), *Biological Anthropology of the Human Skeleton*. Second Edition. New York: Wiley-Liss, pp. 117–147.

Schaefer, M., S. Black, and J. Scheuer. (2009). *Juvenile Osteology*. London: Academic Press.

Scheuer, L., and S. Black. (2000). *Developmental Juvenile Osteology*. London: Academic Press.

Scheuer, L., and S. Black. (2004). *The Juvenile Skeleton*. London: Elsevier Academic Press.

Schmeling, A., R. Schulz, B. Danner, and F. Rosing. (2006). The Impact of Economic Progress and Modernization in Medicine on the Ossification of Hand and Wrist. *International Journal of Legal Medicine* 120 (2006): 121–126.

Schmeling, A., W. Reisinger, D. Loreck, K. Vendura, W. Markus, and G. Geserick. (2000). Effects of Ethnicity of Skeletal Maturation: Consequences for Forensic Age Estimation. *International Journal of Legal Medicine* 113 (2000): 253–258.

Schour, I., and M. Massler. (1941). The Development of the Human Dentition. *Journal of the American Dental Association* 28 (1941): 1153–1160.

Schutkowski, H. (1993). Sex Determination of Infant and Juvenile Skeletons. I. Morphological Features. *American Journal of Physical Anthropology* 90(2): 199–205. DOI: https://doi.org/10.1002/ajpa.1330900206.

Scott, A., S. MacInnes, N. Hughes, T. Munkittrick, A. Harris, and V. Grimes. (2023). A Bioarchaeological Exploration of Adolescent Males at the 18th Century Fortress of Louisbourg, Nova Scotia, Canada. *Bioarchaeology International: Emerging Adolescence* DOI: https://doi.org/10.5744/bi.2022.0007.

Scott, A. B., and T. K. Betsinger. (2021). Reproduction in the Past: A Bioarchaeological Exploration of the Fetus and Its Significance. In S. Han and C. Tomori (Eds.), *The Routledge Handbook of Anthropology and Reproduction*. DOI: https://doi.org/10.4324/9781003216452.

Scott, R. M., and S. Halcrow. (2017). Investigating Weaning Using Dental Microwear Analysis: A Review. *Journal of Archaeological Science: Reports* 11(2017): 1–11. DOI: https://doi.org/10.1016/j.jasrep.2016.11.026.

Shapland, F., and M. Lewis. (2013). Brief Communication: A Proposed Osteological Method for the Estimation of Pubertal Stage in Human Skeletal Remains. *American Journal of Physical Anthropology* 151(2): 302–310. DOI: https://doi.org/10.1002/ajpa/22268.

Shapland, F., and M. Lewis. (2014). Brief Communication: A Proposed Method for the Assessment of Pubertal Stage in Human Skeletal Remains Using Cervical Vertebrae Maturation. *American Journal of Physical Anthropology* 153(1): 144–153. DOI: https://doi.org/10.1002/ajpa.22416.

Skoglund, P., J. Stora, A. Gotherstrom, and M. Jakobsson. (2013). Accurate Sex Identification of Ancient Human Remains Using DNA Shotgun Sequencing. *Journal of Archaeological Science* 40(12): 4477–4482. DOI: https://doi.org/10.1016/j.jas.2013.07.004.

Smith, A., L. Reitsema, A. Fornaciari, and L. Sineo. (2023). Exploring the Effects of Weaning Age on Adult Infectious Disease Mortality among 18th–19th Century Italians. *American Journal of Human Biology* DOI: https://doi.org/10.1002/ajhb.23864.

Sofaer, J. (2007). Engendering Children, Engendering Archaeology. In T. Insoll (Ed.) *The Archaeology of Identities: A Reader*, pp. 87–96. New York: Routledge.

Sofaer, J. (2011). Towards a social bioarchaeology of age. In S. Agarwal, and B. Glencross (Eds.), *Social Bioarchaeology*. Oxford: Blackwell, pp. 283–311.

Solari, A., A. M. Pessis, G. Martin, and N. Guidon. (2020). Fetal Bioarchaeology: A Case-Study of a Premature Birth from Burial 2 in Toca do Enoque (Middle Holocene, Northeastern Brazil). *Childhood in the Past* 13(1): 8–19. DOI: https://doi.org/10.1080/17585716.2020.1738629.

Spake, L., and H. Cardoso. (2021). Interpolation of the Maresh Diaphyseal Length Data for Use in Quantitative Analyses of Growth. *International Journal of Osteoarchaeology* 31(2): 232–242. DOI: https://doi.org/10.1002/oa.2942.

Stewart, N., G. Molina, J. Issa, N. Yates, M. Sosovicka, A. Vieira, S. Line, J. Montgomery, and R. Gerlach. (2016). The Identification of Peptides by nanoLC-MS/MS from Human Surface Tooth Enamel Following a Simple Acid Etch Extraction. *Royal Society of Chemistry Advances* 6(66): 61673–61679. DOI: https://doi.org/10.1039/c6ra05120k.

Stewart, N., R. Gerlach, R. Gowland, K. Gron, and J. Montgomery. (2017). Sex Determination of Human Remains from Peptides in Tooth Enamel. *Proceedings of the National Academy of Sciences of the United States of America* 114(52): 13649–13654. DOI: https://doi.org/10.1073/pnas.1714926115.

Sutter, R. (2003). Nonmetric Subadult Skeletal Sexing Traits: A Blind Test of the Accuracy of Eight Previously Proposed Methods Using Prehistoric Known-Sex Mummies for Northern Chile. *Journal of Forensic Science* 48(5): 927–935.

Tanner, J. (1962). *Growth at Adolescence*, 2nd Edition. Oxford: Blackwell.

Tanner, J. (1986). Normal Growth and Techniques of Growth Assessment. *Clinics in Endocrinology and Metabolism* 15(3): 411–451.

Tanner, J., M. Healy, H. Goldstein, and N. Cameron. (2001). *Assessment of Skeletal Maturity and Prediction of Adult Height (TW3 Method)*. London: Harcourt Publishers.

Tanner, J. M., R. H. Whitehouse, N. Cameron, W. A. Marshall, M. J. R. Healy, and H. Goldstien. (1983). *Assessment of skeletal maturity and prediction of adult height (TW2 method)*. Cambridge, MA: Academic.

Temple, D. H. (2020). The Mother–Infant Nexus Revealed by Linear Enamel Hypoplasia: Chronological and Contextual Evaluation of Developmental Stress Using Incremental Microstructures of Enamel in Late-Final Jomon Period Hunter Gatherers. In R. Gowland and S. Halcrow (Eds.), *The Mother-Infant Nexus in Anthropology*. Cham: Springer, pp. 65–82. DOI: https://doi.org/10.1007/978-3-030-27393-4_4.

Temple, D., and A. Edes. (2022). Stress in Bioarchaeology, Epidemiology, and Evolutionary Medicine. In K. A. Plomp et al. (Eds.), *Paleopathology and Evolutionary Medicine*. Oxford: Oxford University Press. DOI: https://doi.org/10.1093/oso/9780198849711.003.0014.

Thompson, J. L., M. P. Alfonso-Durruty, and J. Crandall (Eds.). (2014). *Tracing Childhood: Bioarchaeological Investigations of Early Lives in Antiquity*. Gainesville, FL: University of Florida Press.

Tierney, S., and J. Bird. (2015). Molecular Sex Identification of Juvenile Skeletal Remains from an Irish Medieval Population Using Ancient DNA Analysis. *Journal of Archaeological Science* 62 (2015): 27–38. DOI: https://doi.org/10.1016/j.jas.2015.06.016.

Tiesler, Vera. (2014). Cultural frameworks for studying artificial cranial modifications: Physical embodiment, identity, age, and gender. In Vera Tiesler (Ed.), *The Bioarcheology of Artificial Cranial Modifications*. New York: Springer.

Ubelaker, D. (1989). *Human Skeletal Remains: Excavation, Analysis, Interpretation* (2nd Edition). Washington DC: Taraxcum.

Ullinger, J., L. Gregoricka, R. Bernardos, D. Reich, A. Langston., P. Ferreri, and B. Ingram. (2022). A Bioarchaeological Investigation of Fraternal Stillborn Twins from Tell el-Hesi. *Near Eastern Archaeology* 85(3): 228-237. DOI: https://doi.org/10.1086/720748.

Uysal, T., S. Ramoglu, F. Basciftci, and Z. Sari. (2006). Chronologic Age and Skeletal Maturation of the Cervicle Vertebrae and Hand-Wrist: Is There a Relationship? *American Journal of Orthodontics and Dentofacial Orthopedics* 130(5): 622–628.

Van de Vijver, K. (2019). Non-adult fracture patterns in Late and Post-Medieval Flanders, a Comparison of a Churchyard and a Church Assemblage. *Childhood in the Past* 12(2): 96–116. DOI: 10.1080/17585716.2019.1638556.

Vlak, D., M. Roksandic, and M. Schallaci. (2008). Greater Sciatic Notch as a Sex Indicator in Juveniles. *American Journal of Physical Anthropology* 137(3): 309–315. DOI: https://doi.org/10.1002/ajpa.20875.

Von Endt, D. W., and D. J. Ortner. (1984). Experimental Effects of Bone Size and Temperature on Bone Diagenesis. *Journal of Archaeological Science* 11(3): 247–253.

Waters-Rist, A. (2023). Stable Isotope Evidence for Breastfeeding and Weaning Variables in Past Populations: Infant and Child Feedings in Ancient Siberian Foragers. In M. Beasley, A. D. Somerville (Eds.), *Exploring Human Behaviour through Isotope Analysis: Interdisciplinary Contributions to Archaeology*. Cham: Springer, pp. 35–73. DOI: https://doi.org/10.1007/978-3-031-32268-6_3.

Watts, R. (2011). Non-specific Indicators of Stress and Their Association with Age at Death in Medieval York: Using Stature and Vertebral Neural Canal Size to Examine the Effects of Stress Occurring During Different Periods of Development. *International Journal of Osteoarchaeology* 21(5): 568–576.

Wesp, J. (2017). Embodying Sex/Gender Systems in Bioarchaeological Research. In S. C. Agarwal & J. K. Wesp (Eds.), *Exploring Sex and Gender in Bioarchaeology*. Oxford: Blackwell, pp. 99–126.

Wheeler, S., L. Williams, P. Beauchesne, and T. Dupras. (2013). *International Journal of Paleopathology.* DOI: https://doi.org/10.1016/j.ijpp.2013.03.009.

White, T., M. Black, and P. Folkens. (2012). *Human Osteology, Third Edition.* Amsterdam: Elsevier Academic Press.

WHO Multicentre Growth Reference Study Group. (2006a). WHO Child Growth Standards based on Length/Height, Weight, and Age. *Acta Paediatrica Supplement* 450 (2006): 76–85.

WHO Multicentre Growth Reference Study Group. (2006b). Assessment of Differences in Linear Growth among Populations in the WHO Multicenter Growth Reference Study. *Acta Paediatrica Supplement* 450 (2006): 56–64.

Wilson, A. (1980). The Infancy of the History of Childhood: An Appraisal of Philippe Aries. *History and Theory* 19(2): 132–153. www.jstor.org/stable/2504795.

Wood, J., G. Milner, H. Harpending, and K. Weiss. (1992). The Osteological Paradox: Problems of Inferring Prehistoric Health from Skeletal Samples. *Current Anthropology* 33(4): 343–370.

Ziegler, E. (2007). Adverse Effects of Cow's Milk in Infants. In C. Agostoni and O. Brunser (Eds.), *Issues in Complementary Feeding.* Nestlé Nutrition Institute Workshop Series Pediatric Program 60: 185–199.

Zuckerman, M. K., and J. Crandall. (2019). Reconsidering Sex and Gender in Relation to Health and Disease in Bioarchaeology. *Journal of Anthropological Archaeology* 54(2019): 161–171. DOI: https://doi.org/10.1016/j.jaa.2019.04.001.

Zuckerman, M., and G. Armelagos. (2011). The Origins of Biocultural Dimensions in Bioarchaeology. In S. C. Agarwal and B. A. Glencross (Eds.), *Social Bioarchaeology.* Oxford: Blackwell, pp. 15–43.

About the Author

Dr. Creighton Avery (she/her/hers) is Assistant Professor (Teaching Stream, LTA) at the University of Toronto Mississauga, and an osteoarchaeologist with Stantec Consulting Ltd. Her research incorporates macroscopic and biochemical approaches to non-adult skeletal remains, particularly as it relates to experiences of children and adolescents in the Roman Empire. She lives in Ontario, Canada with her partner and pup.

Cambridge Elements ☰

Current Archaeological Tools and Techniques

Hans Barnard
Cotsen Institute of Archaeology

Hans Barnard was associate adjunct professor in the Department of Near Eastern Languages and Cultures as well as associate researcher at the Cotsen Institute of Archaeology, both at the University of California, Los Angeles. He currently works at the Roman site of Industria in northern Italy and previously participated in archaeological projects in Armenia, Chile, Egypt, Ethiopia, Italy, Iceland, Panama, Peru, Sudan, Syria, Tunisia, and Yemen. This is reflected in the seven books and more than 100 articles and chapters to which he contributed.

Willeke Wendrich
Polytechnic University of Turin

Willeke Wendrich is Professor of Cultural Heritage and Digital Humanities at the Politecnico di Torino (Turin, Italy). Until 2023 she was Professor of Egyptian Archaeology and Digital Humanities at the University of California, Los Angeles, and the first holder of the Joan Silsbee Chair in African Cultural Archaeology. Between 2015 and 2023 she was Director of the Cotsen Institute of Archaeology, with which she remains affiliated. She managed archaeological projects in Egypt, Ethiopia, Italy, and Yemen, and is on the board of the International Association of Egyptologists, Museo Egizio (Turin, Italy), the Institute for Field Research, and the online UCLA Encyclopedia of Egyptology.

About the Series

Cambridge University Press and the Cotsen Institute of Archaeology at UCLA collaborate on this series of Elements, which aims to facilitate deployment of specific techniques by archaeologists in the field and in the laboratory. It provides readers with a basic understanding of selected techniques, followed by clear instructions how to implement them, or how to collect samples to be analyzed by a third party, and how to approach interpretation of the results.

Cambridge Elements

Current Archaeological Tools and Techniques

Elements in the Series

Archaeological Mapping and Planning
Hans Barnard

Mobile Landscapes and Their Enduring Places
Bruno David, Jean-Jacques Delannoy and Jessie Birkett-Rees

Cultural Burning
Bruno David, Michael-Shawn Fletcher, Simon Connor, Virginia Ruth Pullin, Jessie Birkett-Rees, Jean-Jacques Delannoy, Michela Mariani, Anthony Romano, S. Yoshi Maezumi

Knowledge Discovery from Archaeological Materials
Pedro A. López García, Denisse L. Argote, Manuel A. Torres-García, Michael C. Thrun

Machine Learning for Archaeological Applications in R
Denisse L. Argote, Pedro A. López-García, Manuel A. Torres García, Michael C. Thrun

Worked Bone, Antler, Ivory, and Keratinous Materials
Adam DiBattista

Infrared Spectroscopy of Archaeological Sediments
Michael B. Toffolo

Retrospective and Prospective for Scientific Provenance Studies in Archaeology
Mark Pollard

Archaeological Wood and Woodworking
Caroline Arbuckle MacLeod

Bioarchaeology of Infants and Children
L. Creighton Avery

A full series listing is available at: www.cambridge.org/EATT

For EU product safety concerns, contact us at Calle de José Abascal, 56–1°, 28003 Madrid, Spain or eugpsr@cambridge.org.

www.ingramcontent.com/pod-product-compliance
Ingram Content Group UK Ltd.
Pitfield, Milton Keynes, MK11 3LW, UK
UKHW060701200126
466637UK00026B/181